George Solomon

The Jesus of History and the Jesus of Tradition Identified

George Solomon

The Jesus of History and the Jesus of Tradition Identified

ISBN/EAN: 9783337417499

Printed in Europe, USA, Canada, Australia, Japan

Cover: Foto ©Lupo / pixelio.de

More available books at **www.hansebooks.com**

THE JESUS OF HISTORY

AND

THE JESUS OF TRADITION

IDENTIFIED

BY

GEORGE SOLOMON

NEW YORK
J. W. BOUTON, 706 BROADWAY
LONDON: REEVES AND TURNER
1880

PREFACE.

THE present age is remarkable for the rise and development of an extraordinary interest in the history of Jesus of Nazareth. The enthusiasm with which this subject is investigated has infected the scientific mind universally, and the questions raised have agitated the thoughts and disturbed the dreams of people of nearly every rank and class over the Christian world.

At the head of those who have contributed to awaken and keep alive this interest stand the names of Strauss and Renan; and to this subject these authors, aided by philosophy, have applied, the one the utmost keenness of criticism, and the other the utmost ingenuity of constructive art. Nevertheless, though both are men of much thoughtful originality, and possessed of that width of vision and range of culture which are due to intense study and profound scholarship, and while the writings of the one are marked by strength and subtilty of dialectic, and those of the other by poetic, almost dramatic, sensibility and power, there is in both a deficiency, if not a total want, of that practical sagacity which is an essential requisite to any trustworthy criticism of matters of fact, such as offer themselves to scientific regard in the debated narratives.

The hypothesis of Strauss, as is known, is that Jesus is the impersonation of an ideal of purely mythic derivation, so that, having existed in idea, he was afterwards conceived to have had a corresponding existence in fact; in which view he is partly supported and partly contradicted by the Church theology, for while this asserts in confirmation that "Jesus was the lamb slain from the foundation of the world," it also asserts in opposition that he was slain again in the flesh when Pontius Pilate was procurator of Judea; that, in other words, the ideal became real. But this theory is unsatisfactory, because it is not historically grounded, and because no authentic historical explanation is supplied to account for the rise and spread of the fervid traditional belief.

Renan's theory, as given in his romantic *Vie de Jésus*, is as fanciful in conception as that of Strauss, and is formed in equal disregard of historical accuracy. His chief interest is in the beauty and sublimity of the moral teachings of Jesus, as these are reported by the four Evangelists, and he refers all in the subject of the story to a central self-consciousness in him, which, he maintains, because it is absolutely human, boldly asserts itself to be equally divine; but he leaves unanalysed certain anomalies of character inconsistent therewith, which contrast darkly with his idyllic picture and detract seriously from its dramatic truth.

Both these theories rather reflect the philosophical opinions of their respective authors than any sound criticism of history, the one being conceived in the spirit of the abstract speculation of Germany, and the other after the romantico-poetic sentimentalism of France, but neither representing or affecting to any material extent the public mind or its movements.

In England these theories have been received with very partial favour, and are not likely to be adopted into the national creed. The English people are intensely conservative, and are prone to look askance on any departure from ancestral belief. For theories of all kinds they have but a cold affection, and will not be persuaded to adopt anything novel, unless it can convincingly show itself to be grounded on the secure basis of fact. It is their respect for this latter quality, or that virtue in things which has power to actualise itself, that has encouraged the author to venture on the present undertaking, and to attempt the proof that the story of the traditional Jesus is a development from a historical root.

Hitherto the traditional accounts have only been explicated in a speculative interest; in these pages the first attempt is made to introduce the Christian world to Jesus as known to history before his figure was distorted by popular belief. It is in no spirit of arrogance this task is undertaken, but rather of unfeigned surprise that the proof the author has to offer, though within the reach of every one, is only now for the first time submitted to the light. That proof he commends to the candid consideration of the reader, concerned only that the novelty of his premises may not prejudice their reliability, and that his arguments may secure an impartial verdict from an intelligent public.

KINGSTON, JAMAICA, 1880.

CONTENTS.

CHAPTER I.

THE present attempt, its boldness and seeming arrogance.—Author's justification and expectation.—Aim of the work.—The accounts of the Messianic age, the traditional and the contemporary.—The business of the historian.—Flavius Josephus, his reputation and historical accuracy, his qualifications and title to regard.—His father a contemporary of the traditional Christ, therefore an authority in regard to the events of the time.—Josephus's own account of himself in his youth.—At school under Banus.—He attaches himself to the Pharisees.—His religiousness and disposition to asceticism.—Interested in the religious sects of his time, he yet ignores Christianity.—His account of these sects: the Pharisees, the Sadducees, the Essenes, and that of Judas of Galilee.—Christianity more or less anticipated by all of these, and specially by one.—Two historical facts established: the existence at the time of only four sects, and the current acceptance of the doctrine of immortality and future retribution.—The sect of Judas and its possible identification with that of Jesus.—The Christian sect not then existent.—Its rise afterwards under traditional reports, ... 1–17

CHAPTER II.

THE so-called apostolical accounts necessarily uncertain.—The most reliable source of information, the trustworthy evidence of a contemporary.—The silence of Josephus inconceivable on the received hypothesis.—Contemporary criticism of the documents, and of the relative veracity and unveracity of their authors.—An objection removed.—The relative credibility of the authorities obvious.—Deference due to the most authentic accounts.—The relation of Josephus and the Evangelical writers to the old biblical accounts.—The dogmatic of the Evangelical writers irrational and unbiblical; their doctrine of the Trinity absurd in itself and dishonouring to God.—No compromise possible between the accounts of the Evangelists and those of Josephus, . 18–26

CHAPTER III.

A SUMMARY contrast between Josephus and the Apostolical writers.—The untrustworthiness of the Evangelical writers certified by their internal and mutual inconsistencies.—Their historical inaccuracy not surprising.—Josephus's opportunities of obtaining information.—His virtual denial of the existence of the Christian sect.—The Evangelical accounts not altogether fabulous.—St. Luke's assertion of their historical truth, and reference to eye-witnesses.—The respective designs of St. Luke and Josephus different.—Agreement, in spite of discrepancies, between the adverse accounts.—Josephus' account of the false prophet slain by Pilate, and Pilate's recall, in which he partly agrees with, and partly differs from, the Evangelical accounts.—Improbability of Josephus omitting all mention of another prophet slain by Pilate, if such existed.—The significance of this silence.—The chronology of the Evangelical accounts necessarily at fault.—Difficulty in these accounts in the matter of Herod and John the Baptist.—Josephus quoted in regard to Herod's incestuous connection with his brother's wife.—Important chronological inferences.—Remarkable coincidences between the contemporary and traditional accounts.—Why the attempt to eliminate the historical element from the merely traditional has never yet been essayed.—This the first attempt.—The idea of drawing a historical parallel strangely new.—The materials within the reach of every one.—A summary of the more obvious parallels.—The author only breaks ground, does not attempt an extended analysis.—Analogy between the accounts given of Banus and that of John the Baptist referred to.—The difficulty of identifying these two removed.—The two quantities to be eliminated to secure a literal agreement between the opposing accounts.—Evidence in the Gospels that they were written after the destruction of Jerusalem.—Manifest delusion on the day of Pentecost in respect to the advent of the last days.—Modern parallel enthusiasms and their confessed deceptiveness.—The temper of the day more tolerant of ancient than of modern pretensions, . . 27–48

CHAPTER IV.

THE author's controversy with hallucination only.—His thesis re-stated.—Two accounts compared in proof.—St. Matthew's and St. Luke's on the birth of Christ.—St. Matthew's account unsupported by even the other Gospels.—Its sum.—Prophecies said by St. Matthew to be fulfilled, which were not.—His account of Christ's genealogy as absurd as his account of his birth is fabulous.—St. Luke's version subversive of St. Matthew's, and more probably correct, as regards date anyhow.—Josephus quoted in confirmation.—

His explanation of the appointment of Cyrenius, and his account of the revolt of Judas and Sadduc.—The rise of the sect of Judas coincident with birth of Christ according to St. Luke.—Inference regarding the age of Christ at the time of Pilate's procuratorship.—Christianity an offshoot of the sect of Judas.—The historical importance of this latter sect.—Its justification in its determined antagonism to the ethnic element, which would merge the divine in the human, and subject God to Cæsar.—Fierce hatred to the domination of Rome as represented in the unjust rule of the procurator.—Josephus's account of the Sicarii and the deceptions of the false prophets.—Rise of the enthusiasm for the kingdom of God, ... 49–64

CHAPTER V.

The Gospel narratives first told by Greeks in Greek.—The writings of Josephus accessible only to them.—The Gospels referable partly to his narrative and mainly to traditional report, conceived under the inspiration of a false philosophy in conflict with the Bible.—Account of the Jewish fanaticism in which the Christian religion took its rise.—The religion of Judas of Galilee professedly grounded in the theocratic idea of Moses.—Its combination with an enthusiasm for liberty and the Messianic idea.—The Jews goaded into fanaticism by the tyranny of their Roman rulers.—Pilate's tyranny.—The false prophet slain by him confounded with the founder of Christianity.—The teaching of Judas and that ascribed to Jesus in the Gospel opposed.—Their idea of Messiah and his claims different.—The Greek writers and Paul accountable for the invention of the God-man dogma.—Josephus's account unaccountably different.—Which to trust.—The issue a historical one.—An inconceivable hypothesis.—The Greek writers sacrificed truth to sentiment, ... 65–76

CHAPTER VI.

Josephus ignored by the Greek writers.—Their method of composition by vicarious statement.—The main plot not of their invention, only the details.—They and Josephus write from different standpoints and for different ends.—The burden of the Greek evangel.—Its doctrine of the Godmanhood stated and viewed as glorifying to the Jewish race, and especially the dynasty of David.—Transfer of David's throne to heaven, and the idea of the establishment there of a new Jerusalem, ... 77–83

CHAPTER VII.

The power of accepted beliefs.—The present spirit of inquiry and the Church's claim.—The irrational quality of Christian dogmatic.—The son of God begotten in eternity and begotten in time.—Conceived and not conceived.—The Logos in relation to him.—His three paternities.—His infancy in relation to his divinity.—His conception.—His humanity only mortal.—His divinity in the tomb.—The uncertain relation of the divinity to the humanity.—The cry on the cross.—His relation to the Holy Ghost.—The doctrine of the divine sonship an essential one in the Christian system.—The Church's faith in mystery and fear of heresy, . . 84–96

CHAPTER VIII.

THE Apostles.—James, the Lord's brother.—The relationship indicated not spiritual, but literal.—Discrepancy between John and Paul as to Cephas.—Cephas and Peter, according to Paul, two separate personages.—A perfect network of inconsistencies.—The question of the subsequent chapters, how the name Jesus was substituted for Judas.—The criticism of the Gospels still very imperfect.—The leading points sought to be established, ... 97–104

CHAPTER IX.

THE Messianic age.—The historian of it.—Its leading idea.—Its commencement with Judas of Galilee.—The fanaticism it led to.—Theudas, but no Jesus.—Impostors under Felix, but no word of Jesus.—The fanaticism leads to violence, all which is on record, and yet no mention of Jesus.—Another impostor under Festus.—A Jesus comes to light at last, preceded by Banus.—Banus probably the original John.—Chronological data.—No Jesus till the reign of Nero.—The sect of Judas, its spirit and aims.—The interest and jealousy with which the Romans regarded the movement.—The enthusiasm exclusively connected with the hope of a Messiah, a hope confined to the Jews, and which died out only with the destruction of the city.—The Jews faithful unto death, ... 105–115

CHAPTER X.

THE procuratorships of Albinus and Gessius Florus.—The historical Jesus appears.—Josephus's account of him.—His character and fateful cry.—Meekness under suffering.—Disappearance and imagined resurrection.—His end, and presentiment thereof.—The enthusiasm he awakened.—His fame.—Prodigies.—Their parallels in the Gospels.—None such in Pontius Pilate period.—The day of Pentecost.—The traditional reports thus historically grounded.—Parallels.—The charge of insanity preferred against the Jesus of the Gospels.—The mother and the son.—An impossible conception.—The Jesus of Josephus the same as that of the Gospels, ... 116–132

CHAPTER XI.

The fatal obstinacy of the Jews during the siege of Jerusalem.—Clemency of Titus.—The literal fulfilment of the prophecy of the historical Jesus.—Its fulfilment due to an unseen agency.—The expectation of the Jews, though erroneous and disastrous, not idolatrous.—The Jews answerable for the idolatry of Christendom.—Their sufferings in consequence.—The Christian Messianic period a huge delusion, with its doctrine of the last days.—The Evangelists in a dilemma in asserting the coincidence of the advent of the Messiah and the latter days.—A reconciliation between Jew and Christian proposed.—The infatuation of the Jews due to the teaching of false prophets, which the historical Jesus denounced.—Jewish antagonism to Christianity due to the exaggerated distortions of tradition.—The Jesus of tradition not the Pontius Pilate deceiver.—The Evangelists wrong in their chronology, not Josephus, ... 133–143

CHAPTER XII.

The Jesus of the Gospels a dual character.—This duality due to a mingling of two personalities.—The main chronological errors in the traditional accounts explained.—The connection supplied by Josephus.—The Pontius Pilate pretender must be set aside as prototype of the traditional Jesus.—The promise of Jesus about his return.—The truth not acknowledged in regard to this, out of respect to expediency.—An apology for the Evangelists.—How the conception of the traditional Jesus developed, beginning with the memory of the martyr of Jerusalem.—Inconsistencies in the portraiture to be expected.—Surprising that a story with so many of these should be accepted.—The two natures present in the traditional Jesus shown in his contradictory teachings.—The character presented not consistently meek and merciful.—An impossible one, clearly referable to two, ... 144–157

CHAPTER XIII.

Archæology a vain refuge.—Fanatical enthusiasms, ancient and modern.—Ancient fortified by penalties.—The bonds relaxing.—The destiny of Christianity in the hands of the English.—The missing-link.—The other Jesus.—Zealous for the law of Moses.—Described by Josephus.—Parallels between him and the traditional one.—His coadjutors and following.—Traces of him in the Gospels.—The source of incongruities in the portraiture of the Jesus as given there, and the malefactor described in them.—Master-error of the traditional narratives, ... 158–179

CHAPTER XIV.

JOSEPHUS and the Galilean Jesus.—The latter a disciple of Judas, whom, in his zeal, he supersedes.—Josephus a sure authority.—His opportunities of knowledge.—Says nothing of Jesus of the Gospels.—His account of his own historical labours.—The false chronology of the Gospels not due to him.—The simplicity of the Evangelists.—Unfair treatment of Josephus's testimony.—A parallel drawn between the Evangelical account and an imagined post-historical account of Napoleon.—The character of Jesus self-contradictory, 180–189

CHAPTER XV.

THE divine element overpowering.—Subtleties and subterfuges resorted to in vindication.—Truth here sacrificed to sympathy.—That found in Josephus.—The Evangelists imaginative authors.—Josephus not to be explained away or spiritualised.—The Herods, grandfather and grandson, confounded.—Original facts.—John the same as Banus.—The Gospels *primâ facie* historical.—The Christian dogmatic and morality not self-derived.—Its plagiarisms.—Parseeism, Hinduism, Judaism appropriated by it.—European constitutionalism enslaved to it.—Bethune English quoted from.—The prophecy about the Virgin misinterpreted.—The Christian dogmatic heterogeneous, and a source of discord, . 190–208

CHAPTER XVI.

THE meek elements and the severe in the traditional Jesus from two different historical roots.—Traces of this.—The meek Jesus the vital germ of tradition.—Too sacred to be criticised.—Presence of a baser element affirmed.—Instances.—The inconsistencies recognised before, but not rightly explained.—The Christian theory of the two natures only speculatively based.—The Messiah to be an earthly king, not a God.—Unscrupulous perversions of prophecy.—Pious frauds denounced as immoral.—The philosophy so supported baseless.—The doctrine of God.—Doctrines, separately false, true when blended into one.—The theology of the Bible opposed; its laws annulled.—Rival Gods.—Jesus represented as both God and less than God.—Christian ethics.—Divinity disclaimed by Jesus.—Sophistry of Canon Liddon.—The divine humbled and the human not exalted.—Judaism spiritually superior to Christianity.—Christianity without scientific frontier.—Developed anomalously.—Not heard of at the time it arose, only long after.—Began in Jewish memories of the meek Jesus, and the signs connected with his appearance.—Evidence that it dates from him; and had no existence before the fall of Jerusalem.—The one speck of error.—Coincidences proving that the Jesus of the Gospels and the Jesuses of Josephus are the same, . . 209–235

CHAPTER XVII.

THE Jews responsible for the fall of the Holy City.—Driven desperate by the false expectation of a Messiah.—Jewish economy supposed to be at an end.—Men's thoughts turned to him who predicted the downfall.—The allegation of an earlier Jesus a sheer anachronism.—Josephus's silence.—The Christian writings not known in his time, or marked private and confidential.—Josephus denies the existence of any sect answering to the Christian.—The mention of the Jesus of the Gospels ascribed to him proved to be an interpolation.—Gibbon adduced in confirmation.—Paul's Epistles written after the fall of Jerusalem, ... 236–253

CHAPTER XVIII.

A REMARKABLE coincidence.—The Pontius Pilate pretender not the Jesus of tradition.—The Messianic enthusiasm hails from Galilee.—Quotation from Gibbon.—Character and principles of the traditional Jesus opposed to those of the meek Jesus.—Evidence of the twofold character.—Contradictory features.—The character not objected to, because deemed divine.—The anointing of Jesus.—Two inconceivabilities.—The record of St. John.—His doctrine of the Logos unphilosophical.—His picture of the New Jerusalem drawn from Josephus's description of the old.—His spiritual Jerusalem of the earth, earthy.—Leaves us in the dark about what concerns us more.—Blunders in earthly matters, yet demands absolute faith in his statements.—His ideas about the employment of the saints in heaven.—Our conclusions confirmed by him.—The historical Jesus.—The failure of the attempt to humanise divinity and deify humanity.—Author's review of his work.—Final remarks, ... 254–282

THE JESUS OF HISTORY

AND

TRADITION IDENTIFIED.

CHAPTER I.

The question, its difficulties and the documents—Josephus, his connections and qualifications—His account of the Jewish sects.

IT is a bold, and not a pleasant or gracious, task to assail and try to undermine old beliefs, and essay to refute what the world has for centuries received as sacred historic truth. Such an attempt will needs be stigmatised by most as both an arrogant and an offensive one. When we take into account the character, learning, and ingenuity of those who have made this subject their earnest study, and whose conclusions thereon have been subjected to the sharpest critical tests, such an undertaking might well seem censurable, unless it shall appear, as we trust it will, that we are forced into the arena in the simple interest of truth.

The general public, moreover, is always reluctant to listen to an obscure writer, and tolerate from him opinions contradictory to those which it has received under the sanction of venerated names in which it has placed implicit trust; and this not only renders the task we have undertaken doubly arduous, but is apt to impart to our enterprise from the outset a certain sense of mistrust. There is, however, to balance this, the reassuring persuasion that comes from deep conviction, such as gives strength to the weakest and courage to the most faint-hearted. This being the feeling which inspires us, we have made up our mind at all hazards to venture on the strife, and we throw down the gauntlet to whosoever may accept its gage, with the assurance that, however much our arguments may be underrated, our honesty of purpose will obtain respect, and that a time is coming when, if not in all particulars, then in the main, the view we plead for will secure assent. Nor will the argument rest in the state in which we leave it; abler minds, it is hoped, will take up the ground we advocate, and array before the world in a more complete and conclusive form the evidence that may be adduced.

It will be our business to show that the history of the events recorded in the Apostolic writings is partly confirmed and partly refuted by a writer who lived contemporarily with the events themselves, whose version, as we maintain, deserves a confidence which ought not to be accorded to traditions that took shape in a subsequent period, and which were avowedly committed to writing after the composition of his contemporary historical account.

The traditional accounts given by the Apostolic

writings of the so-called Messianic age are not altogether fancy pictures. The chronology is very seriously at fault, but certain main points are substantiated by the great contemporary writer referred to, though they occupy a less imposing position in his pages, and are all but hidden in the relation of other events, which he deemed it of greater importance to record,—never dreaming for a moment that the posterity for which he wrote would be deluded, as it has been, by its faith in writings which were written long after, when no witnesses survived to contradict them or confirm their truth.

It is not possible for any historian, however careful and circumspect, to anticipate and forecast the delusions of a subsequent age. He discharges his duty and performs the service imposed upon him, if he faithfully record the facts and incidents as they happened, after diligent study of documents and sifting of the evidence within his reach. It is his business, indeed, to record and weigh the delusions of the age of which he writes, whether his own or any preceding one, in order to hand down to subsequent generations a truthful account of its vices as well as its virtues, its superstitions and shortcomings as well as its heroic achievements in word or act; but he is nowise responsible for the use posterity may make of his faithful narrative, whether they turn it to good or to bad account. Historians, indeed, who write for their own generation, are, as a rule, more careful to withhold unpalatable truths than those who address themselves to a subsequent one, but they cannot be silent in regard to events that were openly transacted, and that, as in the case before us, also challenged, and on high grounds too, the attention of all. In professing to relate the history of the time, they cannot leave untold what is known to all their contemporaries, and at the same time lay claim to, still less obtain credit for, historical fairness and veracity.

Of all the ancient historians whose works have come down to us, there is no one who has a reputation for historic justice and impartiality superior, or even equal, to Flavius Josephus. In his own days he was respected at once for his sagacious, veracious intellect, his immense learning, his wide experience of affairs, and his unbiassed love of truth: as he himself expresses it, "neither concealing anything nor adding anything to the known fact of things." He did what in him lay to clear the minds of his countrymen of false ideas of their past history, and made it a point of conscience to transmit to posterity a faithful record of contemporary events.

He challenged his own world, while the witnesses of the facts related were still alive, to impeach the accuracy of his own version, and he did so for the express purpose of guarding posterity against being deceived by the numerous spurious accounts in circulation, whose falsehoods were known to him. Nay, he even ventured in vindication to enter the arena of literary disputation; and he not only vanquished his adversaries, but made good his point, and in so doing afforded the most absolute proof it is possible for subsequent generations to have of unimpeachable integrity and veracity, as well as distinguished fitness for the work he undertook in behalf of his own and after generations. His qualifications for this task, as well as his success in its accomplishment, thus expressly vouched for by his own contemporaries, and through them to us, are sufficient to give weight to his writings, which afford the most abundant evidence, such as no other record of the period possesses, of the most thorough integrity and intelligence, truthfulness of purpose and reliability of account. Is it not surprising, then, seeing that Josephus possessed such pre-eminent qualifications, and that he is by express definition the historian of the Messianic age,—about the events of which there has been more disputation than about those of any other period of history,—that no inquiry has ever been instituted or analysis attempted to establish a parallel, if any, between his account of the time and that of those chroniclers who have since his day gained the ear of Christendom,—a time on the memory of which more is alleged to depend than on the memory of any other in the recorded traditions of the world? This fact is surely warrant enough for the present venture, and alone justifies, and may excuse, any attempt, however rude in form, to broach the subject and break ground upon it. And this we do with the firm persuasion that the author referred to is the one reliable historian of the place and period to which the events in question relate, and that it is, at lowest, but fair *his* voice should be heard and *his* vote taken in so weighty a discussion.

Matthias, the father of Josephus, was a man of eminence in the Jewish state and a contemporary of Pontius Pilate; and it is thus the son, in his account of his times, speaks of his parent:—

"Now, my father Matthias was not only eminent on account of his nobility, but had a higher commendation on account of his righteousness; and was in great reputation in Jerusalem, the greatest city we have."

This notice of his father, as regards his position at least, is borne out by the fact of the high appointment in Galilee afterwards conferred upon Josephus himself. There is other evidence of the most satisfactory kind to show, further, that Matthias was connected by family with those who had held the high-priesthood; that he lived in the days, as we have said, of Pontius Pilate, and must therefore, according to Apostolic writings, have been a contemporary of Jesus Christ. He must accordingly have been, not only a witness, but an active participant in those great events which, according to the same authorities, in those days, owing to their marvellous character, astonished the Jerusalem world. He must, if their account is correct, have seen or known of the rent in the Temple occasioned by the earthquake which is said to have occurred when Jesus was crucified. He must have known the doctrine of Jesus as taught by himself in his frequent preachings both in and out of the Temple. He must have familiarly known those about the Temple whose diseases were miraculously cured by Jesus, and of the thousands who, with more or less of rapt enthusiasm, as these authorities assure us, followed him as, in the regard of some, "the desire of all nations," and of others, "the consolation of Israel." His knowledge of the occurrences of the time could not, owing to his position, have been less than that of the common people, not to say the very women and children of the district. Indeed, all the inhabitants of Jerusalem must have either seen or heard of those wonderful miracles which are recorded as the distinctive badge of the Prophet of Nazareth and the pledge of his Messiahship.

This eminent man, connected as he was with the priesthood too, whose calling brought him into interested relations with every religious revolutionary movement, could not have been ignorant of the new religion, ushered in, as it was, and supported by such miraculous manifestations as a new revelation by its founder, who took such high ground, too, as to deliver over to eternal pains all who did not believe in his word and accept himself as the nation's and the world's Redeemer. Nor could he have been unfamiliar with the character assumed by, and the events recorded of, the Apostles; of the great power conferred upon them by Jesus, and exercised by them in their public preachings and acts. What is more, he must have been a witness of and have shared in the dismay of the city on that Friday when, as related by the Apostolic records, for the three hours Jesus hung on the cross the heavens were darkened.

Is it credible that the father should have been familiar with all this, and the son know nothing of it? that this diligent and faithful historian of the period should have been ignorant of what his own father knew as an actual eye-witness? Or could the father, had he wished, have concealed from the son what was known to the entire generation? Is it conceivable that the Christian sect could have existed in Judea, and its tenets been embraced by his countrymen, without the knowledge of Josephus, who lived in their midst, and who was precisely of that turn of mind to take the deepest interest in a movement which bore so directly on those very political and religious, as well as philosophical, questions which agitated the time, and which he himself held of such importance as a thinker, a statesman, and a Jew?

Let us hear Josephus himself in regard to his sympathies and opportunities, and remark how in early life he displayed those very religious proclivities and habits which the Gospels themselves say prepare the heart for the acceptance of the religion they teach, of which, however, he says nothing.

"I was," he says, "myself brought up with my brother, whose name was Matthias, for he was my own brother, by both father and mother; and I made mighty proficiency in the improvement of my learning, and appeared to have both a great memory and understanding. Moreover, when I was a child, and about fourteen years of age, I was commended by all for the love I had to learning; on which account the high-priests and principal men of the city came then frequently to me together, in order to know my opinion about the accurate understanding of points of the law. And when I was about sixteen years old, I had a mind to make trial of the several sects that were among us. These sects are three:—The first is that of the Pharisees, the second that of the Sadducees, and the third that of the Essenes, as we have frequently told you; for I thought that by this means I might choose the best, if I were once acquainted *with them all;* so I contented myself with hard fare, and underwent great difficulties, and went through them all. Nor did I content myself with these trials only; but when I was informed that one whose name was *Banus* lived in the desert, and used no other clothing than grew upon trees, and had no other food than what grew of its own accord, and bathed himself in cold water frequently, both by night and by day, in order to preserve his chastity, I imitated him in those things and continued with him three years. So when I had accomplished my desires, I returned back to the city, being now nineteen years old, and began to conduct myself according to the rules of the sect of the Pharisees, which is of kin to the sect of the Stoics, as the Greeks call them."

It is not too much to say that Josephus in this gives evidence of a strongly religious turn of mind. His natural instincts, we see, early led him to investigate minutely the claims and tenets of the separate sects of his day, in order to adapt or adjust himself to the one he might, after conscientious study, find to be the best entitled to his support.

Nor does he object, but positively incline, to an ascetic life of a sort, though not required by the ritual of Moses; nay, he actually for three years, out of a religious instinct, embraced a species of monasticism not unlike that of John the Baptist, the so-called forerunner of Christ. And in all this we see no trace of any dogmatic prejudice, but, on the contrary, a quite unprepossessed state of mind, and an ingenuous endeavour from the first to know and deal justly by each several religious sect. How comes it, then, that he utterly ignores all mention even of the Christian sect, though what he says was written after the fall of Jerusalem, long after the recall of Pontius Pilate, under whose procuratorship the chief act in the Christian drama is said to have taken place? Is it rational to suppose that so painstaking an inquirer and accurate a writer, surrounded by the Christian sect too, whose marvellous history had, according to the Apostolic writings, from the time of Pontius Pilate become a very byeword for honour or reproach in every home of Judea, should not only never name that sect at all, but that he should have committed himself to the rash and erroneous assertion that only three sects of philosophy existed in the country? Can we believe that the Christian sect was in existence at this period at all?

To convince our readers of the desire of this historian to furnish the fullest particulars of all the sects of philosophy that flourished at the period, it will be enough to introduce here an extract or two to the purpose from his works. In Book xviii. of the "Antiquities," chap. i. §§ 2–6, he writes as follows :—

"The Jews had for a great while three sects of philosophy peculiar to themselves; the sect of the Essenes and the sect of the Sadducees, and the third sort of opinions was that of those called Pharisees; of which sects, although I have already spoken in the second book of the Jewish War, I will yet a little touch upon them now.

"Now, for the Pharisees, they live meanly, and despise delicacies in diet; and they follow the conduct of reason; and what that prescribes to them as good for them, they do; and they think they ought earnestly to strive to observe reason's dictates for practice.

"They also pay a respect to such as are in years; nor are they so bold as to contradict them in anything which they have introduced; and when they determine that all things are done by fate, they do not take away the freedom from men of acting as they think fit; since their notion is, that it hath pleased God to make a temperament whereby what He wills is done, but so that the will of man can act virtuously or viciously. They also believe that souls have an immortal vigour in them, and that under the earth there will be rewards or punishments, according as they have lived virtuously or viciously in this life; and the latter are to be detained in an everlasting prison, but that the former shall have power to revive and live again; on account of which doctrines they are able greatly to persuade the body of the people; and whatsoever they do about divine worship, prayers, and sacrifices, they perform them according to their direction; insomuch that the cities gave great attestations to them on account of their entire virtuous conduct, both in the actions of their lives and their discourses also.

"But the doctrine of the Sadducees is this: That souls die with the bodies; nor do they regard the observation of anything besides what the law enjoins them; for they think it an instance of virtue to dispute with those teachers of philosophy whom they frequent. But this doctrine is received only by a few, yet by those still of the greatest dignity; but they are able to do almost nothing of themselves; for when they become magistrates, as they are unwillingly and by force sometimes obliged to be, they addict themselves to the notions of the Pharisees, because the multitude would not otherwise bear them.

"The doctrine of the Essenes is this: That all things are best ascribed to God. They teach the immortality of souls, and esteem that the rewards of righteousness are to be earnestly striven for; and when they send what they have dedicated to God into the Temple, they do not offer sacrifices, because they have more pure lustrations of their own; on which account they are excluded from the common court of the Temple, but offer their sacrifices themselves; yet is their course of life better than that of other men, and they entirely addict themselves to husbandry. It also deserves our admiration, how much they exceed all other men that addict themselves to virtue, and this in righteousness; and indeed to such a degree, that as it *hath never appeared among any other men*, neither Greeks nor barbarians, no, *not for a little time; so hath it endured a long while among them.* This is demonstrated by that institution of theirs, which will not suffer anything to hinder them from having all things in common; so that a *rich man enjoys no more of his own wealth than he who hath nothing at all.* There are about four thousand men that live in this way; and neither marry wives nor are desirous to keep servants, as thinking the latter tempts men to be unjust, and the former gives the handle to domestic quarrels; but as they live by themselves, they minister one to another. They also appoint certain stewards to receive the incomes of their revenues, and of the fruits of the ground; such as are good men and priests, who are to get their corn and their food ready for them. They none of them differ from others of the Essenes in their way of living, but do the most resemble those Dacæ who are called Polistæ (dwellers in cities).

"But of the fourth sect of Jewish philosophy *Judas the Galilean* was the author. These men agree in all other things with the Pharisaic notions; but they have an inviolable attachment to liberty, and say that God is to be their only ruler and lord. They also do not value dying any kinds of death, nor, indeed, do they heed the deaths of their relations and friends, nor can any such fear make them call any man lord; and since this immovable resolution of theirs is well known to a great many, I shall speak no farther about that matter; nor am I afraid that anything I have said of them should be disbelieved, but rather fear that what I have said is beneath the resolution they show when they undergo pain; and it was in Gessius Florus's time that the nation began to go mad with this distemper, who was our procurator, and who occasioned the Jews to go wild with it by the abuse of his authority, and to make them revolt from the Romans: and these are the sects of Jewish philosophy."

The majority of Christians, forming probably more than nineteen-twentieths of the whole, have ever been under the delusion that the doctrine of the immortality of the soul, and the severe ascetic morality, which comes out in opposition to the ways of the world, enjoined in the Apostolic writings, together with the generous communism and self-abnegation which are blended in the same description, had their first origin in Jesus and his peculiar dogmatic teachings. The spirituality which scorns the vanities and pomps of the world, the spirit of meekness, and charity, and devotion, together with the brotherly love which induced the rich to give up all their possessions and share them with the poor, are all referred to the same root and deduced from the same example. That contempt of death and that spirit of martyrdom in the cause of morality and religion, with the related virtues, which tend to impart such a sublime character to the Christian faith, and have established for it a claim on the respect and reverence of so many noble people, are assumed to have originated in the teachings of Jesus, and to have drawn their inspiration from Christianity; whereas, in reality, this wonderful spirituality and moral virtue originated among and was practised by a sect of the Jewish race, the one single principle of whose religious creed was submission to God as their only king, and whose zeal and devotion under the power of this simple belief were such as to demonstrate the hollowness of the common Christian conceit that such deep and reverent love as Christianity inculcates can only exist in the hearts of those who worship the name and accept the divine authority of Jesus Christ. This is an answer to those theologians who advocate, on the weak ground of expediency, the necessity of upholding the Christology of the Church, on the idle presumption that the renunciation of that doctrine would cut away the mainstay of the Christian faith, and that without it Christendom would lapse into the grossness of paganism or the indifference of an atheistic creed; as if faith in a Divine Being, and therefore a Divine Providence, would cease altogether if we once let drop the divinity of Christ—that is, the Trinity in Unity of orthodox belief.

But apart from all this, the quotations just made from Josephus clearly establish two historical facts. The first is, that there existed in Judea in the days of Josephus only four religious communities, viz., the Pharisees, the Sadducees, the Essenes, and the sect founded by Judas the Galilean; each of which is so described as plainly to show that, while the peculiar Christianity of the Church had no existence in any one of them, there is in one or another a greater or less approximation to the Christianity that is said in the New Testament report to have existed in the days of the Apostles: a distinction which it is necessary to draw; for those who now profess the Christian creed do not practise that asceticism to which we call attention as distinguishing alike the practice of the Essenes and that of the new sect which was led on by Judas the Galilean. The second fact which these quotations establish is this: That the *doctrine of the immortality of the soul, and that of reward or punishment in a future world for a virtuous or vicious life in the present, did not originate with Jesus,* and that, if professed by him, as is alleged by the Apostolic writers, they are not originally attributable to him, but must have been simply *adopted by him* from these sects, and they are not, therefore, as alleged, new divine revelations.

Now, the Apostles are represented to have been Galileans, and to have asserted that there was a new sect *founded in Galilee by Jesus*, while Josephus asserts there was a new sect *founded in Galilee by Judas*. The only difference in this respect between the two accounts lies in the distinction between the name *Judas* and the name *Jesus*, and some commentators deem this distinction so slight as to define the one to be equivalent to the other. If, therefore, we were to affirm the identity of these two, the facts of history might well seem to warrant the deduction; for Josephus, as we have seen, mentions only one new sect as having arisen in his day, and if *Judas* and *Jesus* are not the same, it would be necessary to conclude that there were either two founders of the one new sect, or else two new sects, contrary to the express testimony of his contemporary evidence.

To our mind there is clear evidence of the truth of Josephus' version, that there were four philosophical sects only,—one of which, as is explained by him, was of recent origin, and founded by Judas of

Galilee; that the Christian sect was not only not recognised at the time, but that it did not exist until a later period; and that it was not till a later period still that the so-called Apostolical accounts were written and received as genuine tradition, those who committed them to writing as authentic having put together what they could gather from far and near of memories presumed to refer back to the direct testimony of eye-witnesses, some of whom ranked as Apostles. As we proceed, positive proof will be adduced to show that this is really the proper view of the case; and we shall, in the course of our argument, furnish testimony to this effect from the so-called writings of the Apostles themselves, which ought at least to have weight with those who have confidence in their saintly character, and thus contribute to bring about a better agreement between the different accounts of the period than has hitherto existed.

CHAPTER II.

Josephus and the Christian Evangelists—A comparative estimate of their respective historic worth.

It is singular with what obstinate perversity the universal Christian world insists, and has all along insisted, on deriving the account of the first beginnings of Christianity from writers of a later age than that in which the related events occurred, from authors who lived in a different country and wrote in an alien tongue, and who knew nothing of what they record except through foreign report from the original scene of the transactions. Information so obtained, and translated, to boot, into foreign ways of thought and modes of expression, and in days, too, when printing was unknown, is not likely to be such as to deserve implicit reliance, particularly when the statements came coloured through various channels from more or less remote sources, not one word of which was grounded on any firmer basis than that of mere hearsay testimony. Surely the most reasonable source from which to obtain a reliable account of the facts alleged would be the history of him who was a contemporary of the Apostolic age itself, who lived on the spot and wrote of the period, who challenged his countrymen to question, and made himself responsible to them for, the accuracy of his statements, and who would have been convicted to his face of falsifying the history of his times if he had not been guided in his description of public events by the strictest regard to truth, and given the most faithful report of occurrences. This indeed is what we may at the least presume in the case of the historian who assumes the task of recording events known to his contemporaries; but it so happens that we have in Josephus one whose accuracy and reliability are vouched for at once by the peculiar cast of his mind, the special opportunities he enjoyed for knowing the facts, and the respect in which his labours were held by his compeers. It is most seemly, therefore, that those who have any respect for historical truth should place the fullest reliance on his narrative, and it is equally reasonable that the writings of those who contradict him should be brought into close comparison with his for any fair and just criticism of the facts of the history. This accordingly is what we purpose doing with the so-called writings of the Apostles, which were of a later origin, and were certainly compiled after the publication of Josephus' account, which includes the same period, and extends not only from the days of Herod the Great, but even comes down to the destruction of Jerusalem by Titus.

If Josephus had not noticed any of the incidents

recorded in the Apostolic accounts, that of itself would have been the strongest presumptive proof of their untruthfulness, since there is, as we plead, on the one hand, unquestionable contemporary evidence of his unimpeachable character as a man, his singular ability as a statesman, and his painstaking accuracy as a historian; and since the events in question, on the other, were not private ones, but such as, on the face of them, were more or less familiar in the province where they occurred to men of every class, from those of the lowest rank up to the Roman procurators and the members of the priestly order, to which Josephus himself belonged, as did his father before him. If Josephus piques himself, or is entitled to pique himself, on any virtue at all, it is on his fidelity and fairness; and it is inconceivable to suppose that he, of all writers, should have dared, in a narrative expressly of his own times, to have omitted to chronicle what was matter of such universal notoriety, or, having done so, that he could have maintained the reputation he had as a historian among his contemporaries.

Now, while we have before us this testimony to the honour and veracity of Josephus handed down by those who both knew him and the history of the period, the very opposite testimony comes to us of the character and qualifications of the Apostles from *their* contemporaries; and it is not a little surprising that the contemporaries of both should have supplied posterity with the necessary data from which to determine beyond reasonable doubt on which side the credibility lies, and which party has the best claim to our confidence. This evidence would not be so complete but for this further significant fact, that the writings of Josephus are unimpeachable for consistency of statement, while those of the Apostles and their followers are notorious for the most reckless disregard of accuracy of assertion.

It is of no avail to object to this, as some might not unnaturally do, that the bad repute in which the Apostolic writers were held by contemporaries is due to the prejudice which existed in the Roman world against the Christian sect in general. To this objection it is enough to answer that there was quite as bitter an animosity at Rome against the Jews as against the Christians, and that if the Romans had suffered themselves to be swayed by this prejudice, it would have affected their judgment of Josephus as well, whom yet they esteemed both an upright man and a faithful chronicler. But we have no need to appeal to contemporary testimony to determine the relative credibility of the authorities in question; we have only to refer to and examine the documents themselves to certify ourselves at first hand of their respective worth and unworth as historical records. In the pages of the so-called Apostolic writings there lie open to the detection of the very dullest contradictions more flagrant and more numerous than ever disgraced any documents laying claim to historical authority, whilst the pages of Josephus show a candour of mind, a coherence of narration, and a conscientiousness of description, which stamp him as entirely worthy of the character for truth he enjoyed in his lifetime; and this is a conclusion the validity of which is enhanced by the fact of his unflinching fidelity to the letter of the Hebrew Bible; so that his version is invariably true to the original account, whereas that of the Apostles is given in such a fast-and-loose way as to shake all confidence in their honesty as men and their veracity as historians, and so amply justify to posterity the judgment of contemporaries. And yet posterity has, in its blind zeal for the faith, shown itself all too indifferent in this instance to contemporary criticism, as if a world of reasonable men alive at the time were not better able to judge of occurrences openly transacted before their eyes than those who have nothing before them beyond what is handed down by a few obscure writers of, at the best, uncertain date; who, though they stand convicted of the wildest vagaries in conceptive belief, and openly forge or falsify quotations from Holy Writ, are, simply because they have been received as sacred from immemorial time, invested with a halo of glory in the hearts of Christian mankind, second only to that with which certain invest the immaculate Madonna and the infant in her arms, conceived by them to be God.

Now, this is not the ordinary way in which matters of fact in other departments of ancient history are decided; we usually pay most deference to the most authentic accounts. How comes it, then, we may well ask, that we treat the so-called sacred history of antiquity differently? Why should the account in highest repute be set aside, and a preference given to those which are distrustfully regarded? The relation in which Josephus and the Evangelical writers severally stand to the old Biblical accounts by itself, shows what historical value is to be attached to their separate narratives. His version is always true to the letter of the original documents, while theirs is infected with the most fanatical misunderstanding of the text and the most perverted misapplications. This is a fact not dependent upon the opinion and judgment of contemporaries, but one of which the documents themselves supply the evidence, and the proof of which we ourselves can verify. Yet, though it is in our power thus to test the judgment of contemporaries in this matter, and ascertain for ourselves the relative value of the documents, we tenaciously cling to the traditional estimate, and unreasoningly prefer the Apostolic report, because it vouches in a certain supernatural and sensational way for notions we cannot otherwise justify, being indeed such as are in outrageous antagonism with the wisdom of ages and the eternal reason of humanity. In proof of this last assertion it is enough to name the doctrine of the Trinity alone, with its preposterous assertion that three are one and one three, that there are three persons in one God.

This doctrine is clearly contrary to the Old Testament one that there is but *one* God, who is one Being, and *no other*, and contrary, therefore, to the religious beliefs recorded in the writings of Josephus. Nor is it of any avail to plead that there is no contradiction involved in this assertion to the ancient faith, inasmuch as the sensational record, as we may call it, confirms the same idea by the express declaration "that there is but one God," and only adds to the original conception the dogma, well named a mystery, of the existence of *three persons* in the one Deity. For, however this may be, it cannot be denied that the doctrine, by supplementing the original absolute assertion of the Creator, virtually declares that assertion defective, seeing that it associates two other beings with Himself of equal essence, as co-workers with Him in that very salvation which He before announced depended on faith in Himself as the one only God. Is not this to charge the Almighty, not only with *suppressio veri*, seeing He is thus made to withhold from faith what yet He afterwards reveals as necessary to faith, but also with *suggestio falsi*, seeing the old revelation of the divine unity in that case offers a false and illusory basis of belief, making, as it does, salvation depend on faith in one Being, when the so-called new revelation makes it depend on the worship of three? What wonder, then, is it that the Apostles should contradict Josephus, when we see that they actually contradict the Creator and make Him belie Himself, who said withal, "I am a jealous God, and I will not give mine honour to another"? For does not such a declaration manifestly announce His purpose to brook no interference with His authority, to accept no divided homage, and to challenge the worship of Himself alone? And when He promised to love those who worshipped *Him only* and obeyed His commandments, how could He require, as the Apostles declare He does, as a further condition, belief in the divinity of the Son and the Spirit, as co-ordinate in power and coequal in majesty with Himself? And thus they not only contradict God, but they actually compromise Him, as being by inference not a God of truth, nor even of mercy; for they teach that He will assuredly cast those into eternal perdition who bind Him to His promise, and serve Him by worshipping and believing *on Him only*.

But our inquiry has a historic and not a theoretic reference—refers to matters of fact and not matters of faith; and though in the latter regard we might advance much in vindication of our main position, we must limit ourselves strictly to the point in hand—the relative historical value of Josephus and the Christian Evangelists. And in this regard one point is very clear, and that is, there can be no compromise between them. Either Josephus has written falsely or they have written falsely; they cannot be both true, for they are in direct conflict. And there is one set of assertions of a historical nature in which, to his vindication, it will be found, as we have just remarked, he is right and they are wrong, and that is in their respective quotations from the Old Testament: his are always genuine and true to the original, while theirs, partly distorted, partly forged, are all more or less taken in a sense and used for a purpose never meant or intended; and this, moreover, to lend to a body of fanatical fictions the air and weight of divine authority. With these preliminary remarks in support of the view which must be taken of the general historical trustworthiness of the two authorities in question, we will now proceed with our inquiry as to their respective credibility in regard to the Christian era and the incidents therewith connected.

CHAPTER III.

The traditional and historical accounts contrasted—Their general agreement in spite of discrepancies in detail.

THUS far we have Josephus introduced to us with a character for historical truthfulness and honesty, which is vouched for by his contemporaries and confirmed by his faithful versions of biblical fact and biblical philosophy. The Apostles, on the contrary, come before us with a reputation among contemporaries for the reverse, a charge which their dishonest and unscrupulous perversion of the ancient and sacred historical Scriptures of the Jewish people too plainly justifies. But the untrustworthiness of the Evangelical writers is not only certified by their perversion, misinterpretation, and abuse of sacred texts; it is established besides by the inconsistency of their statements and the discrepancy of their accounts with one another. And this fact alone—which is a notorious one—might well lead us, were there no other, to expect greater discrepancies still between them and Josephus. It would be surprising indeed if their statements did not conflict with his. Indeed, it may be broadly charged against them, to their discredit as historians, that they are in conflict with the Bible, in conflict with the voice of reason, in conflict with the science of logic, in conflict with the historian of their time, and, finally, in conflict with one another. Nor is it surprising that they should be so inaccurate in their historical statements; for they wrote on hearsay, and the history of the events they relate they gathered, as they themselves avow, from traditions which they received from more or less coloured sources, whilst Josephus had opportunities of obtaining information from the records of the day and from the most authentic witnesses, his own father, mother, and brother having been contemporaries of Pontius Pilate, and he himself in daily association with the ruling families in Jerusalem. He was afterwards governor of Galilee, too, and as such must have had access to all the public archives. He must, if they existed, have been familiarly acquainted also with the younger contemporaries of Jesus, his Apostles, and the generation that immediately succeeded. He must, moreover, have seen springing up around him the Christian churches, and their growing congregations of worshippers, and been aware of the great and wonderful faith they professed and deeds they performed; and yet he deliberately says, and sets it down as authentic unchallengeable history, that while there were three sects of ancient date, there was only one of recent origin, the one *founded by Judas of Galilee.* If the Evangelical accounts be true, Josephus must have written this in the very teeth of the Christian community rising up everywhere under his eyes, and that in terms which challenged his contemporaries to deny and in any way question the truth of his statements.

While, therefore, it is not to be supposed that a set of men, situated as the Evangelists were, and dependent upon merely traditional reports, could supply an accurate historical relation of the events, and it is unreasonable to expect of them the historical reliability of statement which we look for and find in an author with the opportunities of Josephus, we are not compelled to conclude thence that the Evangelical accounts are altogether fabulous. They could not have grown up except on some basis of fact, coloured though that was, so as to be almost invisible, by the superstition it was adduced to support, and the religious creed of which it was supposed to be the revelation. Indeed we find one of the Evangelists, St. Luke, expressly insisting that the Christian gospel is grounded on fact, and referring to the evidence of testimony in proof of its reality and the credibility with which it is regarded. His words are these:—" Forasmuch as *many have* taken in hand *to set forth in order* a declaration of those things which are most surely believed among us, even as they delivered *them unto us*, which from the beginning were eye-witnesses and ministers of the word ; it seemed good *to me also*, having had perfect understanding of all things from the very first, to write unto thee in order, most excellent Theophilus, that thou mightest know the certainty of those things wherein thou hast been instructed."

Here we see the object of the author is not to write a history of the times, but only to relate a statement of events in them to bear out a belief in that in which Theophilus and others also *had been instructed;* and then, in point of fact, there follows a relation of incidents in the bearing professed, although these are in the main positively contradicted by the historian of the period, who writes, not in support of any particular theoretic belief in which his readers had been instructed, but to portray such an image of the time as would be true of it to the end of the world. Each writer has his own particular design; St. Luke's and that of the many who had taken it in hand, being to historically vindicate a given creed, whereas Josephus' was to chronicle, from the best authorities, in the interest of no sect, the political and religious aspects of his own times and those of his father. Thus it happens we have before us, from his pen, a narrative such as will bear out the view we take of the case, commencing with the time of Pontius Pilate, and extending to the end of the war in the fall of Jerusalem; and our readers will be asked to remark how close an agreement there is as to general statements between his relation of events and that of the compilers of the orthodox narratives, despite the too obvious discrepancies between them otherwise in historical detail and the philosophy of religion. To bear out this theory of the case, we must quote pretty largely both from the Apostolic writings and from those of Josephus; and we will commence with the latter:—In Book xviii. of the "Antiquities," cap. 4, § 1, he says:—

"But the nation of the Samaritans did not escape without tumults. The man who excited them to it, was one who thought lying a thing of little consequence, and who contrived everything so that the multitude might be pleased. So he bade them get together upon Mount Gerizim, which is by them looked upon as the most holy of all mountains, and assured them, that when they were come thither, he would show them those sacred vessels which were laid under that place, because Moses put them there. So they came thither armed, and thought the discourse of the man probable; and as they abode at a certain village, which was called Tirathaba, they got the rest together to them, and desired to go up the mountain in a great multitude together. But Pilate prevented their going up by seizing upon the roads with a great band of horsemen and footmen, who fell upon those that were gotten together in the village; and when it came to an action, some of them they slew, and others of them they put to flight, and *took a great many alive, the principal of whom,* and also the most potent of those that fled away, *Pilate ordered to be slain.*"

Then in Section 2 he adds:—

"But when this tumult was appeased, the Samaritan senate sent an embassy to Vitellius, a man that had been consul, and who was now president of Syria, and accused Pilate of the *murder* of those that were killed; for that they did not go to Tirathaba in order to revolt from the Romans, but to escape the violence of Pilate. So Vitellius sent Marcellus, a friend of his, to take care of the affairs of Judea, *and ordered Pilate to go to Rome to answer before the Emperor to the accusation of the Jews.* So Pilate, when he had tarried ten years in Judea, made haste to Rome, and this in obedience to the orders of Vitellius, which he durst not contradict; but before he could get to Rome, *Tiberius was dead.*"

In this narrative we see that Josephus partly agrees with and partly differs from the Evangelical accounts, for he represents Pilate as having involved himself in trouble in consequence of causing the death of a man who was a mere religious fanatic and had no political designs, while he says nothing whatever about, and does not even name, the crucified king, whom, as alleged, thousands followed with their hosannahs, and who was celebrated throughout Judea for his startling oracles and his still more startling works; thus agreeing with the Apostles in charging Pilate with the murder of a prophet, but disagreeing with them in not identifying him with the Christ. Upon which one is naturally tempted to ask, Is it reasonable to suppose for a single moment that Josephus would have omitted to record the doings or mention the name of Christ, when he condescends to refer to this obscure individual, who, though he had many followers, cannot be compared with the *founder* of a religious sect, and one, too, endowed with such attributes as are claimed by and conceded to the founder of the Christian religion? And are we, by combining the Evangelical accounts with his, to conclude that there were *two prophets slain by Pontius Pilate*, one the great character whom they portray, of whom Josephus gives no account, and the other the one whom he alone mentions? Is it possible that, in the short period during which Pilate was procurator of Judea, two characters should have appeared who deluded the people—one who wrought wonders and established a new religious belief, the centre of which was the divine sacredness of his own person, the other an insignificant fanatic, who established no new creed, and was celebrated for no deed of any note—and that both should have been slain by him, the death of the one calling forth no protest, whilst that of the other provoked an appeal to the Emperor? Is it conceivable that the accurate and truthful historian of the day should so distort the magnitude of events as to single out for remark this temporary figure, and say nothing at all of the remarkable personage, the circumstances of whose miraculous career, according to the Evangelical accounts, from its commencement to its close, amazed his contemporaries into a new faith, which gave birth to a new life and a new fellowship in life, and took shape in visible communities called churches, and not only say nothing of him, but virtually deny, in the face of men alive, the living witnesses to his reality, that he ever existed, by express assertion that the only sect which originated in his day was that of Judas of Galilee?

If there were no other evidence that the Jesus of

the Gospels was not slain by Pontius Pilate, that the Christian sect had no existence at the time these Gospels allege, that the miracles, therefore, on the faith of which this sect took its rise, are a mere fable, to an ingenuous mind one would think this silence of Josephus would appear amply sufficient. It is plain that in his day the so-called Apostolic writings did not exist, and that the Christian religion and Church must have first taken shape only at a subsequent period. It will be our business by and by to render probable, if not to demonstrate, this proposition, that the Christian faith and the Christian documents were based upon events and characters as *chronicled by Josephus himself*, so disguised, however, and distorted by tradition, as, except under very careful analysis, to be hardly recognizable as identical.

The chronology of the Apostolic writings cannot well be expected to be other than inaccurate. Considering the necessarily traditional sources of information from which they are derived, it is very natural to suppose that they should differ as they do in this particular from Josephus, as well as contradict each other; and indeed from their own statements it is obvious, for one thing, that the events narrated, if they occurred at all, must have done so at a later period than the date assigned to them. For instance, the death of John the Baptist is recorded as follows:—

Matthew xiv. 1–13:—" At that time Herod the tetrarch heard of the fame of Jesus, and said unto his servants, This is John the Baptist; he is risen from the dead; and therefore mighty works do shew forth themselves in him. For Herod had laid hold on John, and bound him, and put him in prison for Herodias' sake, his brother Philip's wife. For John said unto him, It is not lawful for thee to have her. And when he would have put him to death, he feared the multitude, because they counted him as a prophet. But when Herod's birthday was kept, the daughter of Herodias danced before them, and pleased Herod. Whereupon he promised with an oath to give her whatsoever she would ask. And she, being before instructed of her mother, said, Give me here John Baptist's head in a charger. And the king was sorry: nevertheless for the oath's sake, and them which sat with him at meat, he commanded it to be given her. And he sent and beheaded John in the prison. And his head was brought in a charger, and given to the damsel: and she brought it to her mother. And his disciples came and took up the body, and buried it, and went and told Jesus. When Jesus heard of it, he departed thence by ship into a desert place apart: and when the people had heard thereof, they followed him on foot out of the cities."

Now, as Herod married Herodias in the last two years of Pontius Pilate's procuratorship, it follows as a matter of course, according to this account, that John the Baptist was alive within this period; and as it is further recorded that John was slain by Herod prior to the death of Jesus, it is plain that this is inconsistent with and subversive of the account the Evangelists give of the slaying of Jesus by Pontius Pilate, in addition to that of the false prophet, which authentic history records took place in the last year of his government.

Nor is it true, as is here asserted, that Herod married his brother Philip's wife, as witness the account of this incestuous affair given by Josephus.

In "Antiquities," Book xviii. cap. 5, § 1, he writes :—

"About this time Aretas, the king of Arabia Petrea, and Herod had a quarrel on the account following : Herod the tetrarch had married the daughter of Aretas, and had lived with her a great while ; but when he was once at Rome he lodged with Herod (not Philip, as is related by the Apostolic writings), who was his brother indeed, but not by the same mother ; for this Herod was the son of the high-priest Simon's daughter. However, he fell in love with Herodias, this last Herod's wife, who was the daughter of Aristobulus, their brother, and the sister of Agrippa the Great. This man ventured to talk to her about a marriage between them ; which address when she admitted, an agreement was made for her to change her habitation, and come to him as soon as he should return from Rome. One article of this marriage also was this, that he should divorce Aretas's daughter. So Antipas, when he had made this agreement, sailed to Rome ; but when he had done there the business he went about, and was returned again, his wife having discovered the agreement he had made with Herodias, and having learned it before he had notice of her knowledge of the whole design, she desired him to send her to Macherus, which is a place on the borders of the dominions of Aretas and Herod, without informing him of any of her intentions. Accordingly Herod sent her thither, as thinking his wife had not perceived anything. Now she had sent a good while before to Macherus, which was subject to her father, and so all things necessary for her journey were made ready for her by the general of Aretas's army, and by that means she soon came into Arabia, under the conduct of the several generals, who carried her from one to another successively, and she soon came to her father, and told him of Herod's *intentions.* So Aretas made this the first occasion of his enmity between him and Herod, who had also some quarrel with him about their limits at the country of Gemalitis. So they raised armies on both sides, and prepared for war, and sent their generals to fight instead of themselves; and when they had joined battle, all Herod's army was destroyed by the treachery of some fugitives, though they were of the tetrarchy of Philip, joined with Herod's army. So Herod wrote about these affairs to Tiberius, who being very angry at the attempt made by Aretas, wrote to Vitellius to make war upon him, and either to take him alive and bring him to him in bonds, or to kill him and send him his head. This was the charge that Tiberius gave to the president of Syria."

Now it is related that Vitellius proceeded to obey these commands of Tiberius, but before he could put them in execution, the intelligence arrived in Jerusalem, where he was on a visit for four days, that "*Tiberius was dead;*" from which it is obvious that these events were contemporaneous with the dismissal of Pontius Pilate, whose retirement from the procuratorship of Judea by the orders of Vitellius took place at the same time, "for before he reached Rome," as we have already quoted, "*Tiberius was dead.*"

It is important for the reader to bear in mind that the differences between Aretas and Herod which culminated in war arose mainly from the discovery by the former of an intention on the part of the latter to divorce his wife, who was Aretas' daughter, which intention was carried into effect by Herod in the last two years of Pontius Pilate's government, in the reign of Tiberius. For if it be true that John the Baptist was first placed in prison because he rebuked Herod for marrying his own brother's wife, and that he was afterwards beheaded out of revenge on the part of Herodias, this deed must have been committed in the last days of the procuratorship of Pontius Pilate; and since, according to the same authorities, Jesus was not crucified until after this event, it will follow that the false prophet who was slain by Pilate during the last year of his administration, and whose murder led to his recall from the government of Judea, was the very individual to whom Josephus, as mentioned above, refers, and not Jesus.

Here we wish the reader to remark, that the agreement, such as it is, for which we argue as existing between the writings of Josephus and those termed the Gospels, extends to the incidents they record, and rarely, except in this instance, to the chronology. The several writers refer in common to the same events in such a way, we think, as to clear up and set at rest the doubts and suspicions, often expressed, that the story of the Gospel writers is entirely fabulous, and not based upon analogous incidents recorded in history. It is true the relation of those incidents by the Evangelists is not reliable as regards the chronology, nor is it identical with that of Josephus as respects the characters of the persons described, their position in life, and other important particulars. Nevertheless, though there is not an exact agreement, there is a remarkable coincidence, as regards the incidents themselves, divested, however, of all superstitious, mythical, and other distortions, which too often not only disfigure, but absolutely conceal the truth from the eyes of posterity. And so much is this the case, that no attempt has yet been made to eliminate from the false traditional accounts the historical basis; nor has it, as far as we know, ever occurred to any one that the facts in request are already recorded in the pages of authentic history. This inquiry, it would seem, has never been essayed, mainly for two reasons. On the one hand, there were those who objected to the credibility of the Gospel writings in a historical reference, contenting themselves with the argument that it was impossible they should be true, since, if they were, their statements would certainly be confirmed by historical proof, and that there were historians extant, of undoubted accuracy, who lived at the time and wrote of the period, and yet were wholly silent about the events in question; and, on the other hand, there were those who accepted the writings as superior to challenge, seeing they were divinely inspired, and to be accepted as such at the very threshold as a first article of belief. This, we apprehend, is the first formal attempt that has been made to refer the traditional accounts to authentic historical records, and we persuade ourselves that the analogy we are about to indicate will strike not a few readers with some surprise, as its first discovery did ourselves.

The real history of Jerusalem and Judea generally has, from the time of Pontius Pilate downwards, remained a sealed book to the English public until a very recent period. The parallel events to which we refer have been known only to those who have made a special study of the period, but, so far as we know, not one of these has drawn attention to the parallel as of any historical significance; and unless he happened to have a theological bent as well, he would not be likely to note, or in any detailed degree, at least, trace, the analogies which run through the traditional and historical accounts, so as to recognise their identity. Not that scholarship is necessary to institute the inquiry and conduct the proof; one has only to read Josephus, as already translated into English, and to study his pages with a judgment unbiassed in favour of any hypothesis and a sincere desire to arrive at the truth.

For, however surprising it seems and is, that after such a sifting as the Gospels have been subjected to, no one has ever suggested even the possibility of a comparison, a parallel does exist, all ready at hand too; and it is open to any one who lists to determine the correspondence, nay, radical identity, between the traditional accounts and Josephus, and to satisfy himself that to the latter we must look to find the true historical basis of the former.

Let us note here a few of the parallels to be met

with which establish this identity. The historical account will be found to agree with the traditional in these respects among others :—

1. They alike affirm the existence of a religious sect, which believed, first, in the immortality of the soul, and, secondly, that rewards and punishments in a future existence are determined by a virtuous or vicious course in this life. Both represent this sect as practising asceticism of a severe order, in renunciation of the pomps and vanities of the world, the rich sharing their wealth with the poor in one common brotherhood, as if they were one family, and calling themselves the children of God.

2. They both record the judicial death, under sentence of Pontius Pilate, of one who claimed to be a prophet of the Lord.

3. Both equally testify to the existence of one *Jesus*, who had under him a following of fishermen and poor people.

4. The Jesus, common to both, had friends and coadjutors in the persons of John and Simon; as also a body of followers who received the law from his lips, and obtained their living in his service.

5. This Jesus, common to both, was betrayed by one of his followers, and, when taken prisoner, deserted by all who formerly clung to him.

6. According to both accounts this Jesus had seventy devoted followers, who travelled from city to city, in the one instance, to hear cases and give judgment, and in the other, to preach and heal diseases.

7. Both speak of Simon and John, his confederates, as having been imprisoned and then released.

8. This Jesus, with his two coadjutors John and Simon, is represented by both as at once a great upholder of the law of Moses and a daring innovator on the accepted national faith.

9. In both Jesus is spoken of as a man possessed and beside himself.

10. In both he predicts the destruction of Jerusalem by the guilt of the Jews.

11. Both mention the crucifixion of three persons at one time, and that, when taken down from the cross, the bodies were begged by one Joseph, who was a councillor, a rich and a just man.

12. Nay, the two accounts agree so far as to imply, if they do not both equally assert, the believed restoration to life of one of the three, and actually affirm the death of the other two.

13. Both refer to signs in the heavens visible to all, one of which was a certain particular star of bodeful import.

14. In both we have accounts of one who falsely promised deliverance to his generation, and who would, he said, one day prevail by his power over the habitable earth.

15. The historical account refers to a commotion at Pentecost, when there was first a quaking felt, then a great noise heard, and then a voice as from a great multitude saying, "Let us remove hence." The traditional accounts refer to a meeting together of

disciples at Pentecost, when suddenly there came a sound from heaven as of a rushing mighty wind, and it filled "the house where they were sitting."

There are other correspondences of a more or less striking character and significant import between the historical and traditional accounts which seem to refer to identical occurrences; and it may fall to a successor in this field of research, of sharper critical acumen and greater skill in sifting and arraying evidence, to complete the identification by an extended analysis and with more elaborate proof. We only break ground, and must content ourselves with pointing out to our readers only the more obvious coincidences. Look for the present at the close analogy there is between the actions and general asceticism of Banus, as already quoted from Josephus' life, and those of John the Baptist. Evidently this Banus was not a disciple of the Christian religion, for Josephus associated with him for three years, and would have mentioned such a circumstance. However, since the chronology of the Evangelists is, and necessarily is, at fault, there is no reason to suppose that he is not the Baptist of their accounts, who here knows no Jesus, or any one supernaturally endowed as he was with miraculous powers and gifts. Indeed, so close is the parallel between the character and actions of these two men, that they would be at once recognised as one but for the chronological discrepancy, which, however, is of not the smallest account, as mistakes in regard to date are throughout the Gospel accounts a never-failing element.

We have a palpable blunder of the very same kind, for instance, in the Acts, in which Paul is represented as appealing to Cæsar *Augustus* in the time of Festus' procuratorship, instead of Nero, who was then Emperor. And, indeed, it lay, as we have said, in the nature of the case—in the manner, viz., in which these accounts were transmitted—that the date should be distorted as well as the events exaggerated; only, unhappily, the distortion and exaggeration are such as to make it often impossible to recognise the parallel between the truth at the basis of the traditional narrative and the facts of history. And yet it is not too much to say that, if we would but consent to treat the Evangelical accounts as of no authority in the matter of *miracle* and the matter of *date*, the most literal and perfect agreement would begin to appear between their version and the strictly historical.

It is clear that the destruction of Jerusalem had taken place before that happened which is recorded in the Acts of the Apostles i. 6. Hence we read there that just before the alleged ascension of Jesus, when his disciples came together, they asked their master, saying, " Lord, wilt thou at this time restore again the *kingdom to Israel?*" For this language certainly implies that Herod was no longer king; that the kingdom had passed into alien hands; and that, in consequence, as the further account testifies, the belief was seriously entertained that the last days had come, when the restoration was to be expected.

In Acts ii. 5-18 we read:—

"And there were dwelling at Jerusalem Jews, devout men, out of every nation under heaven. Now, when this was noised abroad, the multitude came together, and were confounded, because that every man heard them speak in his own language. And they were all amazed, and marvelled, saying one to another, Behold, are not all these which speak Galileans? And how hear we every man in our own tongue, wherein we were born? Parthians, and Medes, and Elamites, and the dwellers in Mesopotamia, and in Judea, and Cappadocia, in Pontus, and Asia, Phrygia, and Pamphylia, in Egypt, and in the parts of Libya about Cyrene, and strangers of Rome, Jews and proselytes, Cretes and Arabians, we do hear them speak in our tongues the wonderful works of God. And they were all amazed, and were in doubt, saying one to another, What meaneth this? Others, mocking, said, These men are full of new wine. But Peter, standing up with the eleven, lifted up his voice, and said unto them, Ye men of Judea, and all ye that dwell at Jerusalem, be this known unto you, and hearken to my words: for these are *not drunken*, as ye *suppose*, seeing *it is but the third hour of the day*. But this is that which was spoken by the prophet Joel: And it shall come to pass *in the last days*, saith God, I will pour out of my Spirit upon all flesh; and your sons and your daughters shall prophesy, and your young men shall see visions, and your old men shall dream dreams: and on my servants and on my handmaidens I will pour out in those days of my Spirit; and they shall prophesy."

Here we see more than the chronology at fault; there is an utter breakdown of the supernatural itself, while the contemporary eye sees in the transaction only a scandal and an offence, a manifestation of mere brain-delirium. For this is no ordinary prophet whose seership misgives him, who assures his hearers, on the perversion of an old vaticination, that the last of the days is come. This is the man to whom it was promised that such infallibility would belong, that the things he might say and the deeds he might do on earth would be endorsed in heaven. And here, on the very first occasion on which we might expect the pledge to be redeemed, the promise turns out to be delusive and the supernatural gift to fail, the prophet being himself misled. The latter days here announced have not only not come, but seem as remote as ever, the changes ahead looming as portentous to-day as in any bygone era, and likely to realise a time before which every other may sink into obscurity. And yet, strange to say, this announcement is received as veridical by many who would scorn the prophecies of such men as Dr. Cumming or Brigham Young, whose judgments of the present and visions of the immediate future seem equally well founded.

The predictions of Brigham Young are accepted by as many enthusiastic disciples as were the words of Simon Peter, and his character is revered by thousands who were witnesses of his wondrous doings. How vain this faith is, is plain to every one but his immediate followers, for all know, except the self-deluded, how fallacious are his declarations. It was with the miracles alleged to have been wrought by him as with those reported to take place every Good Friday in different parts of Europe, and the other day among the Mecca pilgrims; the witnesses and vouchers were people not competent to test their validity, and their testimony was therefore worthless. Every sensible person is ready to give this reason why these miracles should not be believed, yet how few there are who are willing to apply the same test to those of Peter or the Gospels generally, as if, forsooth, which is the case with them, such as are recorded after the event were worthier of credit than those attested at the time of their occurrence. Most are quick enough to distrust and repudiate modern deceptions and delusions, however accredited, but they are quite as ready to accept ancient ones, however discredited, because associated with honoured names and venerable ideas, and lest, by conceding them, they should loosen the basis of old institutions, and open the floodgates of unsettling revolution. It is owing to this circumstance alone that the Christian world has come to regard the declaration of Peter as a divine announcement, otherwise the conclusion of those who heard them, or rather witnessed the excitement in which they were spoken, would not appear so preposterous. Anyhow, however it was with Peter, no sober person will believe that in this occurrence the words of Joel were fulfilled, and that the last of the days had come. All but the prejudiced will admit that here is no supernatural gift, no supernatural vision, but mere human misapprehension and misinterpretation, or rather projection into the historic sphere of an ancient illusion and delusion. So that we see here how little faith we have to put in the supernatural claims as well as the chronological accuracy of the Evangelists, and what reason we have to distrust both the miraculous and the historical representations of the New Testament.

CHAPTER IV.

The Birth of Christ—Luke's account of it preferred to Matthew's—Prior existence of the Sect of Judas, and its relation to Christianity.

AT this stage we cannot help feeling and expressing anew our sense of the arduousness and seeming arrogance of the task we have imposed on ourselves, for we are about to invade the sacred precincts of accepted history, and to rudely challenge the asseverations of a currently-believed divine report. We feel that in attempting to demonstrate the stupendous error under which the Christian world has for ages been deceived, we are assuming a bold front, and that there is need we should protest anew with what reluctance we essay the task and venture to dispute the conclusions of so many generations of learned and gifted people. Will our readers believe us that it is solely in the interest of truth we have taken up the pen, and that the war we wage is not with our fellow-men, but only with certain hallucinations which we think mislead them? Our thesis is that the Apostolic writings, while not without an ascertainable basis in authentic history, are, to fortify a certain dogmatic interest, fraught with statements of a historical nature that are palpably and outrageously false.

In proof of this position let us call the reader's attention to the two accounts that are given in Matthew and Luke's Gospels respectively of the birth of Christ.

In Matthew ii. we read :—

"Now when Jesus was born in Bethlehem of Judea, in the days of Herod the king, behold, there came wise men from the east to Jerusalem, saying, Where is he that is born king of the Jews? for we have seen his star in the east, and are come to worship him. When Herod the king had heard these things, he was troubled, and all Jerusalem with him. And when he had gathered all the chief priests and scribes of the people together, he demanded of them where Christ should be born. And they said unto him, In Bethlehem of Judea; for thus it is written by the prophet, And thou, Bethlehem, in the land of Juda, art not the least among the princes of Juda: for out of thee shall come a governor that shall rule my people Israel. Then Herod, when he had privily called the wise men, inquired of them diligently what time the star appeared. And he sent them to Bethlehem, and said, Go and search diligently for the young child; and when ye have found him, bring me word again, that I may come and worship him also. When they had heard the king, they departed; and, lo! the star which they saw in the east, went before them, till it came and stood over where the young child was. When they saw the star, they rejoiced with exceeding great joy. And when they were come into the house, they saw the young child with Mary his mother, and fell down and worshipped him; and when they had opened their treasures, they presented unto him gifts; gold, and frankincense, and myrrh. And being warned of God in a dream that they should not return to Herod, they departed into their own country another way. And when they were departed, behold, the angel of the Lord appeareth to Joseph in a dream, saying, Arise, and take the young child and his mother, and flee into Egypt, and be thou there until I bring thee word; for Herod will seek the young child to destroy him. When he arose, he took the young child and his mother by night, and departed into Egypt; and was there until the death of Herod; that it might be fulfilled which was spoken of the Lord by the prophet, saying, Out of Egypt have I called my Son. Then Herod, when he saw that he was mocked of the wise men, was exceeding wroth, and sent forth and slew all the children that were in Bethlehem, and in all the coasts thereof, from two years old and under, according to the time which he had diligently inquired of the wise men. Then was fulfilled that which was spoken by Jeremy the prophet, saying, In Rama was there a voice heard, lamentation and weeping, and great mourning, Rachel weeping for her children, and would not be comforted, because they are not. But when Herod was dead, behold, an angel of the Lord appeareth in a dream to Joseph in Egypt, saying, Arise, and take the young child and his mother, and go into the land of Israel; for they are dead which sought the young child's life. And he arose, and took the young child and his mother, and came into the land of Israel. But when he heard that Archelaus did reign in Judea in the room of his *father* Herod, he was afraid to go thither; notwithstanding, being warned of God in a dream, he turned aside into the parts of Galilee. And he came and dwelt in a city called Nazareth, that it might be fulfilled which was spoken by the prophets, He shall be called a Nazarene."

Here we have a story *prima facie* of a very fabulous complexion, and one not only unauthenticated by the strictly historical narrative of the period, but of which not even a trace or feature is to be found in any of the other traditional accounts. It is in substance this: That the moment of the birth of Jesus was announced by a star to wise men from the *east;* that by their report of the event not only was Herod troubled, but *all Jerusalem along with him;* that Herod, to compass the child's death, slew all the innocents about Bethlehem; that the parents of the child, being divinely warned of this, fled with him to Egypt; and that they remained there till Herod's death, and did not return till the accession of Archelaus. Now in this account we first of all have announcements made regarding the child, and then prophecies applied to him which were never fulfilled. He never was king of the Jews; never ruler over Israel; and never, as the angel Gabriel in Luke's account promised, ascended the throne of his father David.* And not only was this prophecy never fulfilled, but there is evidence within the traditional accounts themselves to show that Herod's sentence was never executed; for had it been, as is here alleged, John the Baptist, who was in the district, and the senior of Jesus by only a few months, would have been among the number of the slain innocents.

* This cannot refer to a heavenly throne, as is argued; for if the throne of David were a heavenly throne, that would place David above God Himself.

The truth is, that not only are these statements inconsistent with fact, and stultified by non-fulfilment; but we have Luke's version to show that, notwithstanding the important services alleged to have been rendered by the star, the infant Jesus had not at that time seen the light, and that the whole second chapter of Matthew is as fabulous as the first, in which the author gives a genealogy of Jesus to prove the fulfilment in him of the biblical prophecy that the Messiah was to be born of David, while, after adducing the proof of this to the satisfaction of all *Christians*, he at the same time, and nearly with the same breath, gravely assures his readers that Jesus had no genealogy at all, but, being born of the Spirit, was without earthly father.

In St. Luke ii. 1–7 we read:—

"And it came to pass in those days, that there went out a decree from Cæsar Augustus, that all the world should be taxed. (And this taxing was first made when Cyrenius was governor of Syria.) And all went to be taxed, every one into his own city. And Joseph also went up from Galilee, out of the city of Nazareth, into Judea, unto the city of David, which is called Bethlehem; (because he was of the house and lineage of David): to be taxed with Mary his espoused wife, being great with child. And so it was, that while they were there, the days were accomplished that she should be delivered. And she brought forth her first-born son, and wrapped him in swaddling-clothes, and laid him in a manger; because there was no room for them in the inn."

This is a very different version from that of Matthew. Here is no gold, frankincense, or myrrh, however acceptable these might have been in the circumstances,—though one could have wished, for the credit of humanity, that the story had told us how some fellow-sojourner in the inn had had pity and exchanged places with the mother and her babe; but we have angels instead in multitudes, announcing the event to a company of shepherds, "keeping watch over their flocks by night," who accordingly, we are told, were the first to discover and make known to others the birth of the child.

That Luke's, and not Matthew's, is the correct version in this case is rendered more probable, from his reference, by way of date, to what is altogether wanting in Matthew's narrative. A tax is always levied by decree, and record kept in the public archives of the date. Without a decree and its publication it would not be lawful to collect it. Now a decree to this effect, with the date of its issue, exists on record, and by it we can verify the period to which Luke's narrative points. Accordingly it so happened, as has been shown by accurate historical research, that the Cyrenian taxation, and, according to Luke, the birth of Christ, took place, not, as Matthew's narrative implies, in the days of Herod, but after the banishment to Gaul by Cæsar Augustus of Archelaus, Herod's son and successor, who had already ruled some time as king, and then for ten years more as tetrarch; so that it is no wonder that the shepherds could not be directed to the star that guided the wise men of the east, although it came and stood over where the young child was, for already thirteen years had elapsed since the appearance of that notable portent. Neither could they judge from the gold, frankincense, and myrrh that had been offered; they were guided by an angel to a certain inn, where they would find the child wrapped in swaddling-clothes and lying in a manger. The shepherds could not meet the wise men of the east nor the wise men of the east the shepherds, although both, as is alleged, were supernaturally led by divinely-sent infallible ministers, and both had been bound upon the exact same errand—the worship of the young child who was to bring glory to Israel and peace to the world. Stars and star-gazers, however, have often deluded the race, whereas angels and a host of angels have never; and so, of the two, if we must choose, we are inclined to adjudge the meed of credibility to Luke's version, the more so that Luke, with some sense of and regard for historical truth, supplies particulars, and mentions not only the period and the region, but the very spot of the occurrence. And if so, what then becomes of the story of the massacre of the innocents in the last days of Herod, when the date Luke gives refers the birth of Jesus to about thirteen years later than the reign of that tyrant? What becomes of the mysterious star which in his time beckoned the wonder-struck Magi out of Arabia until it stood over the place where the child lay? And what an anachronism it is to run back the Christian era to the last years of Herod's reign!

In proof that Archelaus reigned as king and tetrarch before the date of the Cyrenian taxation, we beg the reader's attention to the following particulars. By the last testament of Herod, Archelaus, his son, was appointed his successor in the kingdom, and Cæsar Augustus was not only nominated the administrator of that instrument, but had the power conferred upon him by the testator of modifying and confirming its provisions. Archelaus succeeded his father in the year one of our era, and commenced his reign with an honest desire to commend his rule to the good-will and favour of his subjects. Before long, however—it is not known how long—disaffection arose, and the Jews, or the chief sect of them, appealed to Cæsar against him, and put in pleadings to his disadvantage. "When," to use the words of Josephus, "Cæsar had heard these pleadings, he dissolved the assembly;" but a few days afterwards he appointed Archelaus, not indeed to be king of the whole country, but ethnarch of one-half of that which had been subject to Herod. In his "Jewish Antiquities," Book xv. chap. 12, § 2, Josephus continues:—

"But in the tenth year of Archelaus's government, both his brethren, and the principal men of Judea and Samaria, not being able to bear his barbarous and tyrannical usage of them, accused him before Cæsar, and that especially because they knew he had broken the commands of Cæsar, which obliged him to behave himself with moderation among them. Whereupon Cæsar, when he heard it, was very angry, and called for Archelaus's steward, who took care of his affairs at Rome, whose name was Archelaus also, and thinking it beneath him to write to Archelaus, he bade him sail away as soon as possible, and bring him to Rome; so the man made haste in his voyage, and when he came into Judea, he found Archelaus feasting his friends, so he told him what Cæsar had sent him about, and hastened him away. And when he was come (to Rome), Cæsar, upon hearing what certain accusers of his had to say, and what reply he could make, both banished him, and appointed Vienna, a city of Gaul, to be the place of his habitation, and took his money away from him."

After all these events, all subsequent to the death of Herod, Cæsar appoints Cyrenius to make a taxation of Syria and Judea, and we arrive at the time when "Joseph, Mary, his espoused wife, being great with child, went up from Galilee, out of the city of Nazareth unto the city of David, and the days were accomplished that she should be delivered of her child."

The historian explains the appointment of Cyrenius as follows :—

In Book xviii. chap. 1, § 1, we read—

"Now Cyrenius, a Roman senator, and one who had gone through other magistracies, and had passed through them till he had been consul, and one who on other accounts was of great dignity, came at this time into Syria, with a few others, being sent by

Cæsar to be a judge of that nation, and to take an account of their substance. Copomius, also, a man of the equestrian order, was sent together with him to have the supreme power over the Jews. Moreover, Cyrenius came himself into Judea, which was now added to the province of Syria, to take an account of their substance, and to dispose of Archelaus's money; but the Jews, although at the beginning they took the report of a taxation heinously, yet did they leave off any further opposition to it, by the persuasion of Joazar, who was the son of Boethus, and high-priest. So they, being over-persuaded by Joazar's words, gave an account of their estates without any dispute about it; yet there was one *Judas a Gaulonite*, of a city whose name was Gamala, who taking with him Sadduc, a Pharisee, became zealous to draw them to a revolt, who both said that this taxation was no better than an introduction to slavery, and exhorted the nation to assert their liberty; as if they could procure them happiness and security for what they possessed, and an assured enjoyment of a still greater good, which was that of the honour and glory they would thereby acquire for magnanimity. They also said that God would not otherwise be assisting to them than upon their joining with one another in such counsels as might be successful and for their own advantage, and this especially if they would set about great exploits, and not grow weary in executing the same. So men received what they said with pleasure, and this bold attempt proceeded to a great height. All sorts of misfortunes also sprang from these men, and the nation *was infected with this doctrine to an incredible degree.* One violent war came upon us after another, and we lost our friends who used to alleviate our pain; there were also very great robberies and murders of our principal men. This was done in pretence indeed for the public welfare, but in reality from the hopes of gain to themselves; whence arose seditions, and from them murders of men, which sometimes fell on those of their own people (by the madness of these men towards one another, while their desire was that none of the adverse party might be left), and sometimes on their enemies. A famine also coming upon us reduced us to the last degree of despair, as did also the taking and demolishing of cities; nay, the sedition at last increased so high, that the very Temple of God was burnt down by their enemies' fire. Such were the consequences of this, that the customs of our fathers were altered, and such a change was made as added a mighty weight toward bringing all to destruction, which these men occasioned by thus conspiring together; for *Judas* and Sadduc, *who excited a fourth philosophic sect among us*, and had a great many followers therein, filled our civil government with tumults at present, and laid the foundations of our future miseries *by* this system of philosophy, which we were before unacquainted withal; concerning which I shall discourse a little, and this the rather because the infection which spread thence among the *younger sort*, who were zealous for it, brought the public to destruction."

It thus appears, on the unquestionable authority of Josephus, that the fourth sect of philosophy mentioned by him as founded by Judas of Galilee took its rise at the time of the Cyrenian taxation, and we have just seen that St. Luke assigns to that same period the date of the birth of Jesus of Nazareth.*

* If the date assigned by Luke for the birth of Christ be correct, it will make Jesus to have been about twenty years of age when Pilate slew the false prophet of whom mention is made in the pages of Josephus, an event which happened in the year 33 of the Christian era. If so,

This new sect sprang into existence before or about the time when, according to Luke, Jesus was born, when the seed which ripened in the ruin of the Jewish state had been already sown and had taken root in the community. That the movement thus originated assumed eventually, under modifications in its spirit and aims, the name of Christianity, there is no reason to doubt. It was, as the historical accounts testify, a religion which, when it was first introduced, was strongly blended with the politics of the day, had throughout a political significance, and tended rather to subvert than strengthen the Roman authority in Judea. The altered attitude this sect assumed towards Rome after the destruction of Jerusalem, in acknowledging in a general way its supremacy, could not fail to obtain for it respect in place of the hatred that was entertained against it, and to be received with all the more favour from the fact that its first initiation arose out of a general patriotic feeling of the Jewish race against the Roman usurper.

The explanation of the philosophy of this sect, as tendered by Josephus, we have given in another place. This explanation must be received as a historical summary of the original philosophical creed and political bearings of the Christian sect, and taken

it follows that Jesus was only twenty when he was crucified by Pilate, whereas the traditional accounts make him to have been thirty-three ; and if he was crucified by Pilate, it follows that there were two conspicuous characters who, during the last years of his procuratorship, fell victims to their religious zeal, of whom authentic history mentions *only* the one, while the Evangelical reports mention *only* the other.

as a point of departure for the comparison, and a basis for the identification, of the traditional and historical accounts.

According to Josephus, this sect had already an existence at the time Luke alleges Jesus was born, and its tenets were professed by multitudes before he opened his lips to speak, or had even the gift of utterance. And this is the sect which we venture to assert eventually developed into Christianity, and which, in the course of its development, when there was more of the Judas than the Christian element in its creed, brought about such seditions and tumults as to divide the Jewish people into opposite factions, at internecine feud with each other, and to strengthen the section that could not brook Roman domination, but regarded it as a curse that would one day bring down on the nation the vengeance of Heaven. However much the rest of the race might receive Augustus, Tiberias, or Caligula as deities, each—for it was virtually that, they thought—as a man-god, the Jews as a body preferred to suffer death and dispersion rather than submit to such a degradation and desecration ; and all who have studied the history of the period will allow that they had too good reason to rebel, considering the rapacity of the Roman procurators of Judea, who vied with each other in their criminal acts of cruelty and oppression. And, indeed, the strife that went on then was a world-strife ; for here we are, after eighteen centuries of confusion and debate, arrayed under the same antagonisms that developed then, the Jewish section uncompromisingly repudiating, and the Christian as uncompromisingly maintaining, the worship of man as God. For, in spite of all the changes that have taken place since —and they have been considerable both in magnitude and moral significance — it is wonderful to note how the Jewish and the Christian philosophies retain to this hour the same essential distinction which has separated the creed of the Jew from that of other races since the beginning, that the modern antithesis between Jew and Christian is radically the same as that which existed of old between Jew and Gentile.

The religious delusions which at this time prevailed and spread everywhere, tending to the disintegration of the Jewish state, contributed to intensify the hatred to the domination of the Roman authority, and stir up a determination to overthrow it and cast off its yoke, while the conservative element became gradually weaker and less able to stem the rising tide of lawless violence and vice. And as the Roman procurators, instead of upholding the cause of justice and order, winked at these proceedings, especially when by such connivance they might promote their own aggrandisement, that government appeared to many more a curse than a blessing, and its removal a dire necessity laid on every Jew who loved the land of his birth and the religion of his fathers.

Josephus relates in "Wars of the Jews," Book ii. cap. 13, §§ 3, 4 :—

"When the country was purged of these, there sprang up another sort of robbers in Jerusalem, which were called Sicarii, who slew men in the daytime and in the midst of the city. This they did chiefly at the festivals, when they mingled themselves among the multitude, and concealed daggers under their garments, with which they stabbed those that were their enemies; and when any fell down dead, the murderers became a part of those that had indignation against them; by which means they appeared persons of such reputation that they could by no means be discovered. The first man who was slain by them was Jonathan the high-priest, after whose death many were slain every day; while the fear men were in of being so served was more afflicting than the calamity itself, and while everybody expected death every hour, as men do in war; so men were obliged to look before them, and to take notice of their enemies at a great distance; nor, if their friends were coming to them, durst they trust them any longer; but, in the midst of their suspicions and guarding of themselves, they were slain. Such was the celerity of the plotters against them, and so cunning was their contrivance.

"There was also another body of wicked men gotten together, not *so impure in their actions, but more wicked in their intentions, who laid waste the happy state of the city no less than did these murderers. These were such men as deceived and deluded the people under pretence of divine inspiration*, but were for procuring innovations and changes of the government; and these prevailed with the multitude to act like madmen, and went before them into the wilderness, as pretending that God would there show them the signals of liberty; but Felix thought this procedure was to be the beginning of a revolt, so he sent some horsemen and footmen, both armed, who destroyed a great number of them."

The account of the appearance at this juncture, and the political influence, *of men who deluded the people under pretence of divine inspiration*, is a notable historical admission, and reveals a condition of things calculated to prepare the mind to receive with less astonishment the Apostolical relation. That the enthusiasm connected with such a state of matters should increase and give birth to others, was natural in the complications which arose and the prodigies which accompanied them. And, accordingly, history records the fanatical excesses that followed, and denounces as deceivers those who, affecting a zealous reverence for liberty, forbade their followers to acknowledge any other authority than the *kingdom of God*, and excluded all human authority except that of their own sacerdotal order, to which they adhered with a tenacity which has hardly a parallel in the history of the world.

CHAPTER V.

The four Greek writers—Their accounts a perversion of biblical truth and historical reality—Mistakes in regard to the reign of Messiah—The rise of this idea.

To the Greeks alone belongs the distinction of having first published to the world the several versions accepted by Christians of the life of the founder of their religion; and what is noteworthy, they were the only people who, before these writings were produced, were cognizant of the works of Josephus. No others could read these works, for they were written in Greek; and they relate, as we have said, all that happened in the so-called Messianic period, from the time of Herod the Great to the procuratorship of Pontius Pilate, and later. In no other tongue are earlier versions of these Gospels to be met with, and these were first presented to the Grecian world in Greek, and not to the Jewish world in Hebrew or Chaldee. The story of the incidents recorded in the Gospel history was confessedly imported from the land of their occurrence to a *foreign* land, and it first saw the light under the guise of a foreign language. The historical groundwork of this story is to be found in the writings of Josephus. That historian's account of the incidents very closely agrees with theirs, only they have brought within a short space a variety of events which he refers to as having happened over a more extended period, and as matters of history rather than as facts in illustration of a peculiar philosophy. If no other land produced the Gospel writings, it is because no other land had at that time the writings of Josephus. If the Greeks had been as ignorant as the rest of the world of these writings, they would not, and could not, have composed the four Gospels. As it is, the Apostolic books are grounded partly on traditional reports and partly on historical statements found in Josephus; only the traditional element has overborne and obscured the historical, and has no doubt caused the statements of these books to be conflicting and contradictory. And they *are* so conflicting and so contradictory that, as has been often remarked, one author not only disagrees with another, but each separate account is full of inconsistencies.

No writings, save and except those of the Holy Bible, have ever made such an impression upon the European world as these have done; and yet no writings contradict the Bible more, while they at the same time affect to be its fulfilment and confirmation. They bear testimony in words to the truth of the Bible, while they advance a philosophy which is entirely opposed to its teaching, and can by no sophistry be traced to it as its germ and root. The

Bible commences a revelation of which they pretend to be the sequel; yet, while the first revelation announces to the world an unalterable moral law, the second abolishes that law, on the ground that it is obsolete; and while the first revelation pronounces God to be a unity, the second represents Him as both a unity and a trinity. That such should be the case, however, is not surprising when we consider that the authors of the second revelation were obscure, at any rate unknown, personages, who were probably Greeks by birth as well as Greeks by language, and that the scenes of their narrative lay not in Greece but in the land of Judea. The story they tell was composed of elements which came to them through the distorting medium of traditionary report and a false philosophy.

As we have seen, the historian of Judea mentions the existence among the Jews of his day of a class of men who stirred up the people against their rulers on the pretence of a commission from the Almighty—mere worthless impostors, who deluded and carried away multitudes, more particularly of the younger and more fiery spirits of the nation. They professed to be animated by a greater reverence than others for God, a holier zeal for the law, and a more genuine patriotism; and all pointed to some great biblical prophecy about the latter days as either fulfilled or on the eve of fulfilment, and that in circumstances than which few more favourable ever offered themselves to foster and promote the work of the deceiver. For everything conspired to favour the delusion imposed upon the age that preceded the period referred to in the Apostolic writings. The religion of Judas of Galilee was embraced by multitudes. The enthusiasm with which this religion was accepted was based on appeals to the patriotism of the people, and this was wrought upon by certain political schemers to compass their own ambitious designs. Nor were the arguments with which these crafty men plied the mob of the day without foundation in the philosophy of their religion. The theocracy of the Jews, as established by Moses, was, it was alleged, a purely divine institution, and the establishment of a merely human authority within it was regarded as an innovation which amounted to its subversion. A kingdom of God upheld only by sacerdotal authority was indeed the Mosaic ideal, and this Mosaic institution underwent a change when a king was chosen and appointed to rule instead of the priesthood, Moses being simply the mouthpiece and minister of this divine order. The philosophy of Judas of Galilee, which reverted to this original idea of the Jewish state as a pure theocracy, could not fail to find amongst the followers of Moses sincere adherents, and it soon took practical shape in a combined determination to shake off the yoke of Roman domination and authority. And the Roman procurators of Judea, by their rapacity and criminal injustice, did what they could to encourage popular revolt and render the public mind a prey to superstitious delusions.

The struggle for liberty, being blended with religion, became a struggle for religious liberty; and the establishment of the kingdom of God on earth as well as heaven was an idea well calculated to inspire a spirit of reverent and zealous devotion. A king of righteousness, of the seed of David, it was proclaimed, was coming to reign over the habitable earth, and all mankind should one day bow before his sovereign authority. All the nations of the earth were about, as predicted, to acknowledge the one true God, and the Jewish people must now, if never before, stand true to their sacred destination, and sternly refuse homage to an earthly lord, still more a foreign despot.

On the one side, political tyranny of the direst kind was practised by the Roman Cæsars and their representatives, the procurators of Judea. Insults were heaped upon the Jewish people and reckless liberties taken with their sacred rites; and these followed each other with alarming rapidity. Each new Cæsar usurped divine authority, and claimed a respect due only to God from a people who were taught to prefer death to idolatry. Each new procurator or ruler ignored the existence of the native tetrarch or king, and scorned his authority as well as spurned his advice, especially when these were exercised in opposition to the commands of the Emperor. The procurators, who sought their own aggrandisement more than that of the province or even Rome, scrupled not to stoop to the meanest machinations to enrich themselves; they even covertly encouraged public plunder and rapine, in the hope of sharing in the spoil. Pontius Pilate, one of these, was removed from the procuratorship, because, to gain his own ends, he had ordered, among other tyrannies, the execution, along with many of his followers, of a false prophet, whose motive for feigning a divine commission seems to have been a wish to exercise a certain hierophantic influence over them by his deceptions. For this offence Pontius Pilate underwent a trial at Rome, and so flagrant was it regarded, that, according to some authorities, he is said to have been found guilty by Roman judges and banished to a remote province of the Empire.

It is this prophet whom the Apostolic accounts christen with the name of Jesus, and make the founder and author of a new religion, which they expound and allege to have been accepted by multitudes. Of this same person Josephus asserts that he was a deluder of the people and a false prophet, and he contradicts the assertion that he was the founder of a new religion by ascribing that honour exclusively to Judas of Galilee, who, as remarked, must have had a considerable following before the date of the birth of Jesus as given by Luke the Evangelist. So that if Luke's account, which ascribes the origin of one sect to Jesus, be as correct as that of Josephus, which ascribes another and prior sect to Judas, it follows, contrary to the express statement of the latter, that two new religions had been founded, and that both had originated in Galilee, which two religions were at the same time almost identical as regards dogma, each propagating a similar scheme of belief and practice, which culminated in one master-idea, that of the kingdom of God to be realized on earth as it is in heaven. For in these respects the teaching of Judas and the teaching of Jesus agree with each other and the original Messianic idea; only the expected Messiah, who was, under the providence of God, to appear on earth and rule, was, in Judas' regard, to be a king of *righteousness* but *not a God;* whereas the Greek historians of the period, since called the Messianic, assert that the prophet who was slain was not only the Messiah, but God Himself; that he had lived on earth in Judea for some thirty-three years, and that the age and the district had been made famous both by the astounding miracles which he wrought himself and his followers in his name after him. They even give an account of signs and wonders, both on earth and in heaven, which accompanied his advent, and marked the period and place of his birth as notable before all other periods of history and places upon earth. Unlike the appearances of the Greek gods in the affairs of men, not his advent only, but his whole career was invested with a halo of divinity. A present God was proclaimed from the Temple, from the tops of the mountains, from the seashore, from cities and villages, in sacred places and secular, before high and low, among all ranks and classes of the Palestine world. At least so four obscure Greek writers in an after age assert; and had they not done so—for Josephus says nothing of it, nor any other contemporary—the world would to this hour have been equally ignorant *of God's visit to earth*, and of the form in which He presented Himself to the eyes of mortals.

These four Greek writers, along with another—Paul—who received a special visit from God after He left the earth, are good enough to inform the world not only of all the particulars of His visit, but of the place it held and the purpose it fulfilled in the divine economy. God made a covenant with God to visit the earth in the form of man on a benevolent enterprise. To save mankind from perdition, it was necessary to break the power of the devil, and in order to effect this purpose, and defeat and destroy the adversary, it was also necessary that God should assume man's nature and die in man's stead. God, being eternal, could not die, but He came in the human person of Jesus, who, it is alleged, founded this new religion; which yet can be historically proved to have existed before he saw the light. But these Greek writers knew better, it seems, what took place in Judea than did the inhabitants of Judea at the time themselves; and yet there is nothing to show how they were better informed, except we assume that the very events occurred of which contemporary witnesses are altogether silent, that the transactions recorded could be done at once *in public and in the dark.* These four Greek writers, however, it would appear, had some private and peculiar sources of information not accessible to the rest of the world. They knew what the devil said to Jesus and what Jesus said to the devil; what took place in secret between the high-priest and the Roman soldiers,—how the latter had been bribed by the former to say that the body of Jesus was taken away by his friends, to deceive the public into a belief that he had not risen, as if such a trick could not have been exposed at once by the reappearance of *Christ alive again* in the midst of his enemies; for it is not said that the high-priests had intimation that Jesus would after his resurrection *hide himself* from the public view, and only show himself again to a few Galileans. Yet, indeed, these Galileans were a favoured people, men, women, and children alike, however humble in rank and worthless in character. It is the most pious men, of stainless life and high repute, who always perform high and even ordinary functions in the holy ceremonies of religion; and the anointing of kings is the appropriate function of those who are revered for their gravity of conduct and high moral and spiritual standing in the community; but according to these four Greek writers, this personage, who claimed to be God, allowed himself to be anointed by a woman who had led a loose life and been an outcast from the most ordinary society; and this act of anointing by such a character is deemed to have made the subject of it holy.

If these four Greek writers speak the truth,

Josephus must have concealed from the world a multitude of events of which his very contemporaries were aware, and which his parents and their contemporaries actually witnessed. Josephus condemns the philosophy which has its outcome in Christianity as propounded by Judas of Galilee, pronouncing it a madness, since it led to issues which were to be absolutely deplored, and gave rise to a delusion that provoked the multitude of the Jews to an insurrection which caused the destruction of the Temple and the sacerdotal authority, and therewith the Jewish national community. No just reason can be given for his calling the founder of that philosophy *Judas* instead of *Jesus*, if he was *not* Judas. Can he be accused of having intentionally altered the name, or did he mistake the one for the other? If he committed such a mistake, had he not the power to rectify it? Was such a mistake likely to be made by him in the face of the Christian community? Could he have committed it, had the Christian religion existed then, with its thousands of witnesses, to attest that not Judas but Jesus was the author of their faith? Could Christianity have had then any existence? Would not those who wrote at a subsequent period, when the living witnesses of the events were all dead, be more liable to commit this error? Either they or Josephus, therefore, misstate the fact. It is for the reader to judge whether they who were foreigners, and lived after the events, or he who was a native of the scene of them, and all but contemporary, was most likely to be in error. Which are we to trust?—the writings of Josephus, which were received as accurate by all parties at the time, and composed with a single eye to historical truth, or the compositions of the four Greek writers, which have no historical weight, and are conceived in the interest of a sect of religion? It is scarcely credible, after a fair and just inquiry into the case, that an honest preference can be given to the latter in the face of the unchallenged reputation of the former for truth and honour.

If it is an ungracious thing to attack a cherished idea because it is a delusion, it is a still more ungracious thing to suppress truth in order to support fiction. History is not history, if it be not true; and if it be not history, it is fable; and if fable, let it be treated as such. Yet in this case historical truth is more important than in any other, for except in fact there is no other basis for a doctrine, or set of doctrines, at once the most momentous and most mysterious that have ever been proclaimed for the acceptance of the world. The whole issue as between Christianity and reason depends upon this: whether it is a fact or not that Almighty God in the form of man lived contemporaneously and in the same district with the parents of Josephus, and whether He, appearing there and then as God, was the founder of the Christian religion, and was called *Jesus of Galilee?* Could such a wonderful event have happened, and so happened,—such as is never related to have occurred at all before in the annals of the world,—without the knowledge of the inhabitants of the district in which the event occurred, without record, or shadow of record, in the contemporary history of the period? Is it conceivable that the knowledge of it was first revealed to four Greek writers, at a subsequent period, living in a foreign land? Is it possible that the miracles accompanying this event, not to mention the miracle *in* the event, should, while professedly open to all, have been kept secret from all, even the most inquisitive, until that late time when the four Greek writers referred to first announced it to the world?

These four Greek writers clearly constructed their narratives as purely traditional accounts, and they sought no opportunity, as they felt no desire, to test the truth of the traditional statements, albeit there lay to hand the history of Josephus as composed by himself in the Greek language. It did not, and could not, occur to them to verify accounts which they were inclined to believe, and did believe, came from eye-witnesses so venerated and venerable. Still it was their duty, as narrators of history, and a history the truth or falschood of which was of such moment to the world, not to have allowed their feelings to overmaster their judgment, and to have weighed well the evidence of other contemporary witnesses.

CHAPTER VI.

The different standpoints of the Greek writers and Josephus—The Greek Evangel, flattering to the Jew—Elevation of the Davidic dynasty—The New Jerusalem.

THE ordinary rules of evidence should not be set aside because the interests involved are of the highest importance. Not the less reason is there in that case, but the more, why the related statements should be put to the test, especially when it is in our power to correct mere hearsay accounts by contemporary ones. The four Greek authors themselves ought to have known that they had departed in their statements from the current reports, and the motive, aim, and end of such contradictions should be given by them. It was their duty, also, to refer to such previous accounts, and to combat those statements to which they take exception.

Yet they never for once refer to Josephus, whose History, embracing the self-same Messianic period as theirs, was already published in the Greek tongue, and must have been well known both to the educated Greeks and the dispersed of Israel among the Greek people. They refer to a multitude of events *referred to by him,* but record them in such disorder as regards date that no two of the narratives correspond together. Indeed, it is not necessary to compare their writings with those of Josephus in order to prove them false, for each, as we insist, not only contradicts another, but each makes statements that are self-contradictory. The dramatic narrative composed by these writers, each more or less in his own way, though it embraces much that is historically true, is extensively blended with sheer fiction; to such an unprecedented extent, that the Christian critic has found it necessary to invent for the proceeding a new name, and call it vicarious statement; that is to say, a statement which, as a general rule, is not to be seriously accepted as truth, but only used in the way of argument for the defence of the Gospel and its peculiar theories. And indeed the Christian apologist is apt to grasp at any weapon by which he can repel attack, so that what is sometimes regarded as vicarious is at other times relied upon as *literally true*, and the alternations, significant as they are, pass unnoticed by many, who are too much overawed by the drama itself to note any inconsistency in the details of it.

It must be conceded that the four Greek writers did not originate the plot of their story, but they altered its incidents very materially, and so shortened the intervening periods as to render their chronology entirely anomalous. The material for the plot was most ample; it was coextensive with the scheme sketched in the Hebrew Bible; only the new composition took liberties, for it introduced elements that were not only discordant therewith, but contradictory. Josephus could have had no object in misstating the facts of history; he does not pretend to be the founder of a new philosophy; he is not even a fanatical adherent of the old; he is of no philosophy except that which loves, seeks, and speaks truth. The four Greek writers are desirous, nay zealous, to found a new sect, with a new philosophy, in support of which they avowedly write their histories. Josephus writes to record facts, not in their bearing on any system, but simply as unprejudiced, unimpassioned statements of actualities. The four Greek writers are wedded to a superstitious belief, and bigotedly intolerant of every other. Josephus could only succeed as a historian, and obtain acceptance for his work, by being dispassionately truthful and impartial. There would have been thousands to accuse him had he written falsehood, and he never would have had the reputation which has come down to our day as the most reliable of all historians. There is this, we allow, to be said in behalf of the four Greek writers: their primary object was not to maintain the dignity of history, but to establish and obtain acceptance for an alleged realised life-philosophy; their primary interest was spiritual, and not scientific. Hence the penalty with which they threaten those who do not adopt their view of things, and the high award they hold out to those who accept their doctrine. Their great and professed aim is to gain proselytes, and they promise to those who believe a final exemption from death and a resurrection of the body, with eternal blessedness in the world to come.

The gospel they preached may be summed up in three propositions :—1. That biblical prophecy had been fulfilled by the actual advent of the latter days. 2. That the Messiah who was to usher in the latter days had actually come. 3. That this Messiah was none other than Almighty God Himself in human form.

This was the burden of the Greek evangel. All that was human of the Messiah was entirely Jewish, and what was not human was divine in the sense of very godhead—the godhead of the God of heaven and earth; only they represent the Jewish element so blended with the divine as to render the Jew in him indivisible from God and God from the Jew. Added to this, they proclaimed a glorious martyrdom of the Jewish humanity, which, in obedience to the wishes of the Creator, offered itself in sacrifice to save the whole human race from eternal perdition. A scheme more flattering to Jewish vanity could not have been devised; it exalted the Jewish race beyond all measure. Nor was the scheme the outcome of an accidental series of events; it had been decreed before time began—was the divine evolution of an eternal purpose. The genealogy of Jesus, of the Messiah, by divine decree from God Himself, brought whole tribes and families of the Jewish race into direct blood-relationship, so to speak, with the Creator.

Henceforth many of them could claim the closest kinship with the Supreme, while all could regard Him as a co-religionist, who had submitted to their ritual and adopted their worship as His. Thenceforth *God* Himself should fill the throne of David, be reckoned as one of his dynasty, and usher in the glory of the latter day. The hero of the drama had to die, as all must die, whether heroes or not; but, that it might not be tragical, the hero should come alive again, and so reviving, reign over the house of David for ever. It was the Jewish humanity alone that was heroic; his divinity could not suffer pain or death, being eternal; and therefore it was the Jewish portion of this man-God that underwent this ordeal, to save, at the expense of his own race, the rest of the world. Once the Divine Being would not, as in the case of Isaac, suffer a father to sacrifice his son, but here He ordained and accepted the sacrifice of His own only-begotten. From of old, according to the Mosaic law, the sacrifice of a human life was an abomination to the merciful God; but now God has changed His nature, and what was once an abomination to Him is as the odour of sweet incense, with which He is well pleased. For these four Greek writers *knew* that this sacrifice was of His appointment, and must needs have the seal of His sanction and complacent regard, and could no longer be an abomination in His eyes. According to this theology, the dynasty of King David was raised to an elevation far above every other in the history of the world, as recorded by these four Greek writers.

F

His latest descendant had revealed himself, not only as Messiah, but as God Almighty, who had, by dying and rising again as immortal, transferred the seat of the house from the Jerusalem on earth to the Jerusalem in heaven. David's line had culminated in deity, and henceforth that line rules the earth from the throne of eternity, and the world's God is of David's issue and David's dynasty. The Greek writers fortify their statements about the transfer of the throne of David from earth to heaven by quotations from the prophets, which, they aver, have this reference; others, not aware of this reference, simply record the events which they knew had befallen this kingdom of David, but say nothing about its translation to heaven. Josephus furnishes his readers with very full particulars of the destruction of the old Jerusalem, and therewith its ancient throne; and one of the four Greek writers (John) has a minute account to give of a New Jerusalem, more glorious and abiding. The one account cannot be contradicted, because it has been realized; the other cannot, because it has not. One thing is evident, that the idea of the *New Jerusalem* did not arise till after the destruction of the old one; otherwise it would have been designated *another* or a *second*, not a *new* Jerusalem. And to bear out this view it is enough to remark that the kingdom of Israel first fell to pieces with the fall of the Holy City and the ruin of the Temple. The question is alleged to have been put to Jesus by his Apostles, when would he *restore* the kingdom to

Israel? Such a question could not have been put into their lips except in retrospect of the downfall of the city.

It is, therefore, reasonable to infer that, as there was still hope for the kingdom as long as the city stood, references in the Gospels to a restoration and a new city point to a date posterior to the destruction of the old city by Titus.

CHAPTER VII.

Christian metaphysics—The miraculous conception—The infant Christ, the dead Christ, and the Divinity—Mystery—Heresy.

THE obstinacy with which old ideas hold their ground against the claims of modern science, and the extent to which they retard the progress of thought, are facts of too common occurrence to have escaped the notice of the scientific observer. So strong is the sway of accepted opinions, that they continue to assert themselves long after they have been scientifically exploded. Often they so fit in with established arrangements that their complete rejection would necessitate something equal to a social revolution, from which people naturally shrink in fear of the consequences. Under the old superstition it is always open to argue,—We know where we are, and we know not where a change may land us; so we cling fast to the old, rather than risk the pain of rupture and readjustment. The past, too, we plead, has stood the test of experience; and it is folly to cast aside the lessons it teaches for a scheme of things which it may be hard to establish, and still harder to reduce to harmonious action. The old, too, is familiar, and it takes a long time to find one's place and play one's part among new acquaintances. Besides, it is a humiliation which few can bear, to confess mistake, and so stand convicted of unreason and folly, and expose themselves to self-reproach and condemnation.

Most men, rather than own themselves wrong in such matters, will take refuge in any fallacy that offers support to their old belief, and hope thereby to escape the consequences of their self-delusion. It is the resource of the ostrich, which, when pursued, digs its head into the nearest bush, and stupidly thinks, because it does not see, it is not seen. But the creed of the Christian Church must sooner or later undergo a radical revision, if it is to maintain its hold over the Christian world. There is at present too determined a search for truth to long hinder the recognition of fallacies, which would have been discovered and discarded long ago but for the trick to which the Christian Church has all along had recourse of persuading its youth from earliest childhood that a belief in them was necessary to prosperity in time and blessedness in eternity. It is not till the understanding ripens, if even then, that doubts arise, amid shrinkings lest the early impressions should suffer damage; and then the mind resorts to subterfuges to dull the shock and reconcile itself to what otherwise it would reject as unreasonable. The grander features in the character of Christ start now into bold relief, and the morality of his teachings; and so the mind relapses into its first prejudices, and loses all power of impartial judgment and doing the justice which Truth demands of all her votaries. In nine hundred and ninety-nine cases out of a thousand, such justice cannot be done; early teachings from loving and venerated lips having instilled opposite opinions, and biassed the affections of the mind before the ripening of the judgment. Every effort, too, is made by the Church to discourage and check all inquiry, not by alleging " that where ignorance is bliss, 'tis folly to be wise," but by affirming the greater sanctity of blind faith than rational conviction; as if there were greater merit in abnegating reason than in submitting to it.

Before we proceed with our main argument, which belongs exclusively to the domain of history, we have deemed it advisable to insert here a paragraph or two in demonstration of a few of the dogmatic absurdities to which the human intellect is committed by the acceptance of the Christian creed.

It is, for instance, abstractly admitted by all mankind that of two utterly opposite statements both cannot be true; the one or the other *must* be false, and both may be; and yet Christianity affirms both thesis and antithesis; that is to say, it denies what itself affirms, and again affirms what it denies. Thus it is a proposition of Christianity and a leading article of its creed that the only-begotten Son of God was begotten from eternity of God the Father; and, again, that this Son was begotten of the Holy Ghost in the year *one* of the Christian era; so that whereas the Holy Ghost proceeded from Jesus before he was Jesus, Jesus also proceeded from the Holy Ghost when he became Jesus. Thus Jesus was begotten in heaven and begotten on earth; in heaven, from eternity, of God the Father, and on earth of the Holy Ghost, 1880 years ago. It is alleged that he went back to heaven *locally* through the atmosphere in a cloud, in the sight of his Apostles. Had he come down the same way, he might have dispensed with the assistance of the Holy Ghost. Thus we have this somewhat inexplicable theory:—There are three persons of the Trinity in heaven, and in order that the second person, the only-begotten Son from eternity, should come down to earth, the third person must interpose, and overshadow the Virgin; but how the action of the third person upon one on earth could translate his companion the second from heaven, we must leave to the learned to guess. At present, we have the explanation of Bishop Pearson, who says that Jesus *was* conceived by the Holy Ghost and *not* conceived by the Holy Ghost; but how this non-conceiving conception of the Holy Ghost can avail to bring down the only-begotten Son to earth, unless he came of himself, the inventive theologian must explain—not we.

Another answer is possible to this question, and we half anticipate it will be offered to relieve it from the difficulties with which it is beset; and that is, that it was the *Logos* which was communicated by the Holy Ghost. But such an explanation would be an outrageous sophism, without the slightest weight, inasmuch as the only-begotten Son of God is alleged to be the second divine person in the Trinity, and equal with God, and, in fact, very God, and worshipped as such; as a being, that is, and not simply an inspiration. Thus, then, we have before us the astounding announcement that the only-begotten Son of God was begotten of God, *was* at once conceived and *not* conceived by the Holy Ghost, and according to the relation of the four Greek writers, was begotten and not begotten of Joseph, his earthly father. He is thus described to have had three paternities:—The first the Creator; the second the Holy Ghost, originally in part proceeding from his own substance; and the third the earthly Joseph, so that he might appear to be of the seed of David, to make good the assertion of Messiahship. Taking all these solemn asseverations together, he had an earthly father and no earthly father; he imparted somewhat of his vitality *to* the Holy Ghost, and received again somewhat of his own vitality *from* the Holy Ghost, in conjunction with the Virgin Mary, who contributed his humanity, which was physiologically perfect, without any human father. This perfect man received from the Holy Ghost a perfection which made him in every sense of goodness, as well as in fact, perfect man and perfect God. The humanity had a maternity but no paternity, and the divinity had no maternity but a paternity. The conception was miraculous and the deity invisible. The being ushered into existence was an infant, so far as humanity was concerned, and that infant contained a divine being, which existed from eternity, so far as the divinity was concerned. But though this divine being was begotten from eternity, he remained in the infant and kept silent, until the infant reached the age of maturity, say thirty years, without discovering himself; and up to the present moment he has kept himself hidden in his fleshly habitation, and become so contented with his narrow abode that he identifies himself with the human being who contained him. Henceforth, then, let it be said that they are one and the same person, the humanity possessed by the divinity and the divinity possessed by the humanity, an incorporeal being one with a corporeal.

And first as regards the human substance. It was not perfect man and perfect God, but it was a perfect infant and perfect God. Before he became an infant this Son of God from eternity hid in the womb of Mary for nine months; but as to whether he was conscious or unconscious, theologians are more at sea than they appear to be on other parts of the problem. We are well assured, however, of his being conscious from eternity up to the time of his incarnation in the divine nature of that unborn babe, and we are to presume that, being eternal, he did not with his incarnation become an imbecile, since it is not supposed that the divine nature sank to the level of human nature. It is impossible to believe that the eternal and absolutely self-conscious ruler of the universe should be bereft of sense and power and remain for nine months unaware of his identity.

Christian theologians allow that the Eternal could not suffer pain or death, but they are silent as regards his helpless state in the womb of the Virgin.

We have before us, then, the assertion that when Jesus was born he had, as an infant, the eternal being within him, with all the wisdom and power which belong to deity. The baby God could not exercise, for he had not, the power of speech, but being an incarnation of the eternal Son of God, he knew all things, while his little humanity knew nothing. Nor could he even conceive an idea, so that the humanity derived no advantage from the indwelling deity, while, on the other hand, deity was crushed under the conditions of humanity and reduced to a nonentity. All this, however absurd it looks, follows as a necessary consequence from the assumption that Jesus was the only-begotten Son of God from eternity, equal to God and very God. Far be it from us to indulge in levity on such a subject, and one which many dear friends look upon as sacred. It is not our analysis of the doctrine that is the cause of the offence; it is the doctrine itself when subjected to the test of reason.

The conception of Mary was a miraculous one, issuing in the birth of Jesus; yet although it was miraculous, the being born was a human being, investing a latent God. The outward casket, Mary's son, because born, was fated to suffer pain and die. Not so the inward deity, which yet could never be seen to be there or to leave, any more than enter, its clayey tenement. Of what became of the unseen God when the body of Jesus died and lay in the tomb, there is no mention; but it is well known to Christians that as soon as Jesus came alive again, the only-begotten Son of God re-entered the restored humanity; that is to say, if he ever left it, for no one ever saw him; and it is not expressly asserted that he quitted the body of Jesus even after its dissolution. Jesus, it is affirmed, could not have raised himself from death, unless the only-begotten Son of God had, by restoring vitality, given him the power to do so; and it is assumed that he was content to abide in that body for ever, and invest it with his own glory. If Jesus be very God, because God incarnated Himself in him, then in him the only-begotten Son of God from eternity is merged and lost to sight. If he should ever come out of Jesus, leaving him to his simple manhood, and take up his abode in some other being, this other being would become God, and Jesus would cease to be God; or, if he could abide in more than one being (which is an idea not alien to Christian dogmatic),* then there would be a corresponding multiplication of gods. But if he should choose to come out of Jesus, and continue to subsist apart, he would resume his original character as a manifest divinity and Jesus cease to be God; only, according to the theologians of the Church, this will not be the case, for they make no distinction between Jesus and the

---

* The only-begotten Son of God from eternity is represented by the Creed to be in the body of Jesus, as also in his soul in Hades.

only-begotten Son from eternity. Their doctrine is that the only-begotten Son from eternity condescended to dwell in the narrow humanity of Jesus, for if he did not dwell within him, Jesus would cease to be God, and if he divested himself of the humanity, then he would cease to be the Messiah; for of the seed of David the Messiah must remain. On the other hand, to be the Son of God, equal to God and very God, necessitates that the only-begotten Son from eternity should dwell for ever in the human body of Jesus, so that once united, the connection between the Son of God and the Son of man can never be dissolved. When the human sacrifice to save all mankind was offered on the cross, it was arranged finally that the human being should be the outward divinity, shutting in everlasting bondage the only-begotten Son of God, who forfeited to this human form all the honours of everlasting *visibility*, and who should become the Son of God, because he was the Lamb slain, and would sit on the right hand of God for ever.

No matter if the Logos left the body of Jesus during the continuance of death,—and of this theologians cannot be certain; it would never do so again —and of that fact theologians are perfectly certain. Therefore it must be concluded that the location of the Logos is to be permanent, and that Jesus shall henceforth be known as the Son of God, and though outwardly known as the Son *of David*, will inwardly contain the Divine Being, thus uniting in one person, not the mere title, but the very essence of God and man, even if not commingled.

The last words of Jesus on the cross are thus given in Matthew xxvii. 46 :—" And about the ninth hour Jesus cried with a loud voice, saying, Eli, Eli, Lama Sabachthani! that is to say, My God, my God, why hast Thou forsaken me?" Theologians have not thoroughly explained these words of reproach that proceeded from the lips of Jesus at his dissolution. They do not account for them by surmising that the Logos then deserted his body, leaving him powerless in his unsupported humanity; still less do they allege that the exclamation was a last dying reproach addressed to the Creator. And indeed such a supposition as this is inadmissible, for this death was matter of covenant between the Father and the Son, and therefore he could not as a willing sacrifice complain of the desertion, if any, which he had to suffer in its execution.

To this it will be answered that this was not the cry of his divinity, but his humanity; that the latter, not the former, was the subject of this agony; which amounts to this, that the Logos, although he covenanted with the Most High to undergo this martyrdom, only fulfilled it by proxy, by entering into a human body without sharing in its humanity, and causing that humanity to undergo this martyrdom instead. The humanity suffered, and the humanity should be honoured ever after, but henceforth, as heretofore, there shall be no distinction, and Jesus shall be known only as the only-begotten Son of God, begotten first by the Eternal from eternity, and begotten afterwards in time, for earthly exigencies, by the Holy Ghost.

Again, it is said the Holy Ghost had proceeded from God the Father and God the Son (a late discovery in Spain), and God the Son was conceived again by the Virgin Mary through the operation of the Holy Ghost. Thus the Holy Ghost would, as previously explained, partly proceed from Jesus before he was Jesus, and Jesus would partly proceed from the Holy Ghost when he became Jesus. It is not, however, to be conceded that Jesus was actually conceived by the Holy Ghost, for learned divines say that he *was* conceived by the Holy Ghost and that he *was not* conceived by the Holy Ghost. And it was really necessary for them to advance this negative, for since he was said to have been begotten from eternity, it occurred to them, as it would occur to any one, that such an assertion was inconsistent with a conception afterwards. The fruit of the conception, however, might be the human body of Jesus, and the only-begotten Son of God, it may be said, came merely down from heaven and took his habitation in that body, and so a mystery was created which, as such, would commend itself to the faith of the unintelligent vulgar.

The identification of the Logos or only-begotten Son from eternity with Jesus Christ is an essential dogma of the Christian system. As we have previously shown, the ages have exhausted their ingenuity to convert this into a vital element of Christian belief, and to gain for it the acceptance of the Catholic Christian world. But genius itself has limits to its power, and is frequently beaten back confounded by the majesty of truth. Sophistry, however ingeniously manipulated, is compelled at times to succumb out of respect to the challenge of truth in the lips of others. Sophistry needs prejudice to uphold it, truth only impartiality of judgment.

Very few of those who embrace Christianity know the full import of its tenets, and the Church in its polemic avoids the treatment of those subjects that only suggest matter of question and afford no edification to belief; and if any signs of scepticism appear, the doubter is quashed by being told that he is saved not by knowledge but by faith. These matters, it is alleged, moreover, are too high for human intelligence to grasp, and they must be dismissed from the mind as belonging to the realm of *mystery*. This last is a potent word to conjure with, and propositions the most contradictory to reason are transformed under its spell into integral parts of a divine philosophy. The fondness of Christian theology for combinations of the kind is indeed remarkable, and it has cultivated this sublime alchemy from the beginning. Thus, in regard to the Mosaic law, it taught that it was both abolished and not abolished, and that the Christian was both bound by it and free from it; and this is, was, and will be enforced and accepted as a mystery, credible by faith because incredible to reason. The crusade against heresy carried on by the Roman Catholic Church is prosecuted with no less vigour by their Protestant brethren. Heretical themselves, the latter will permit no further heresy. The ultimate standard being at length attained, the final compromise has been struck, and a creed is offered in the name of Christ all bristling with inconceivabilities. Whatever fallacies have been accepted are to remain as henceforth undeniable, and it will be better for mankind to believe in a myth than to be heretical in the eyes of the Church. A heretical mystery is repudiated as a myth, while an orthodox myth is reverenced as a mystery. The word myth is as offensive to the Christian theologue as the word mystery is the reverse, and he is ever fain to build his mysteries on facts, which he finds not difficult to do, seeing how his facts are compounded. A great bugbear from of old is heresy.

CHAPTER VIII.

The Apostles—Peter and Cephas—Confusion confounded—Judas, the brother of James—Relationship between Jesus and John—Imperfect criticism—Recapitulation.

THE four Greek writers do not agree as to the names and persons of the Apostles. In St. Luke's Gospel and the Acts we have one Thaddeus, whereas the other Gospels mention instead an Apostle of the name of Judas, distinct from Judas Iscariot. According to two of the accounts, this Judas is the brother of James, and all four writers mention the two Jameses. One of these is represented to be the brother of John, while the other, according to the two authorities mentioned, is the brother of Judas. These two Jameses, the brother of John and the other who is designated by Paul James the brother of the Lord, are both alleged to have been killed by the authorities in Jerusalem.

But what we especially desire to bring before the reader's attention is the fact of this last being called the Lord's brother.

The reason given by some for this designation is very unsatisfactory. It is alleged by them that the expression does not imply that he was a blood-relation, but only that he was a brother in the *faith,* as one of the Apostles. If so, it is difficult to understand why he should be so signalised when the rest of the Apostles are identified under mere natural relationships, one as the brother of John and another as the brother of Simon Peter. It is natural, therefore, to conclude, that as the designation was used literally in regard to them, it was so used also in regard to him. The difficulty is further enhanced by additional particulars which are supplied us by Paul and John. Paul thus writes to the Galatians, chap. i. 18-20 :—" Then after three years I went up to Jerusalem to see Peter, and abode with him fifteen days. *But other of the Apostles* saw I none save *James, the Lord's brother.* Now the things which I write unto you, behold, before God, I lie not."

There being two of the same name among the Apostles, it was necessary to distinguish one from the other; and how is this done? By identifying one of them as James the Lord's brother. It could not be because he was an Apostle he was accounted the Lord's brother, but because he was literally a blood-relation. No other conclusion can be reasonably drawn from the language; and as the fact is vouched for by Paul on oath, it should be accepted as authentic, at least by those who have faith in him as a reliable authority. Fourteen years after this visit to Peter, Paul again went up to the Holy City, where, as he says, he a second time met the same

Apostle, along with others. But let us read his own account, to see how, by the comparison of it with that of John, the *Greek writers are in this matter at variance with him no less than with one another.* Paul states, Galatians ii. 8, 9 :—

"For he that wrought effectually in *Peter* to the apostleship of the circumcision, the same was mighty in me toward the Gentiles: and when *James, Cephas, and John*, who seemed to be pillars, perceived the grace that was given unto me, they gave me and Barnabas the right hands of fellowship, that we should go unto the heathen, and they unto the circumcision."

Hear what John says, chap. i. 35-42 :—

"Again, the next day after, John stood, *and two of his disciples;* and looking upon Jesus as he walked, he saith, Behold the Lamb of God! *And the two disciples heard him speak,* and they followed Jesus. Then Jesus turned, and saw them following, and saith unto them, What seek ye? They said unto him, Rabbi (which is to say, being interpreted, Master), where dwellest thou? He saith unto them, Come and see. They came and saw where he dwelt, and abode with him that day; for it was about the tenth hour. One of the two which heard John speak, and followed him, was Andrew, Simon Peter's brother. He first findeth his own brother Simon, and saith unto him, We have found the Messias, which is, being interpreted, the Christ. . . . And when Jesus beheld him, he said, *Thou art Simon, the son of Jona; thou shalt be called Cephas, which is, by interpretation, a stone.*"

Here the reader will remark it is alleged that Simon Peter and his brother Andrew were originally disciples of John the Baptist, who is the cousin of Jesus, but who affects not to know him except as the "*Lamb of God*," as though he knew him only in his heavenly and not at all in his earthly relationship. These disciples leave the service of John the Baptist to become the Apostles of Jesus, while Jesus is seemingly unaware of their ever having been the Apostles of John, or of his ever having pointed him out to them as being the Lamb of God. How men can boast of their being eye-witnesses, and yet not be accurate as to whose Apostles they were, implies a very grave and wilful deception.

According to John's narrative, Jesus, without being publicly told, knows at once the name of Simon, and says, "*Thou shalt be called Cephas.*" Now, though there is no mention here of the name of Peter, there is no doubt, from the relationship given, that Peter is meant, and that he is here called Cephas; and yet this Cephas is unaccountably sundered from the person of Peter, and the two names become by and by the names of *two separate* persons; for Paul, as we have seen, testifies that James, Cephas, and John (the same *John* who testifies that *Cephas* is Simon), were all seen by him in the flesh as distinct personalities, and "gave him and Barnabas the right hands of fellowship." Here then is one of the Evangelists furnishing an account which Paul declares upon his oath as an eye-witness to be false. We do not know to whom to award the meed of credibility in this case, with such an experience of their historical inaccuracy and with such estimates of their unreliability handed down to us by their contemporaries. As, however, Paul's statement is given on oath, and he speaks of the actual presence on the occasion referred to of John, Peter, and Cephas, we are forced into the belief that Peter and Cephas must have been two separate individuals, and not, as in the account of John, two names for one and the same person.

In the course of our inquiries we find it impossible to pursue a direct line, in consequence of the confusion of contradictory statement which we everywhere encounter. Hence it is we are obliged at this stage to make what might seem a digression, and to quote from Matthew. In Matthew xvi. 13–17 we read :—

"When Jesus came into the coasts of Cæsarea Philippi, he asked his disciples, saying, Whom do men say that I, the Son of man, am? And they said, Some say that thou art John the Baptist; some, Elias; and others, Jeremias, or one of the prophets. He saith unto them, But whom say ye that I am? And Simon Peter answered and said, Thou art the Christ, the Son of the living God. And Jesus answered and said unto him, Blessed art thou, Simon Barjona; *for flesh and blood hath not revealed it unto thee, but my Father which is in heaven.*"

This last statement brings us face to face with a perfect network of inconsistencies. The revelation which is here declared, not to have been revealed by flesh and blood, is asserted by John the Evangelist to have been *revealed* to this very Simon and Andrew his brother by *John the Baptist*, who was literally the *flesh-and-blood cousin of Jesus himself*, while the account given above by Matthew of the first introduction of Andrew and Simon to Jesus implies that neither was introduced by the Baptist, if they even were disciples of his at all. And not only do these two writers contradict each other in regard to the introduction of Peter to Jesus, and the manner of the revelation of the latter to the former, they are equally opposed in their statement of the occasion when the Cephas or rock-title was conferred. John says it was when John the Baptist introduced him to the Messiah on the banks of the Jordan; Matthew that it was when the revelation was first made by God in heaven. So that it appears, and it is that it may appear we mention it, these documents are historically unreliable; that step aside where we may, we come upon nothing but confusion and contradiction absolutely bewildering.

But it is another inquiry which in connection with this presses for answer. Why is James called both the Lord's brother and that of Judas? Can it be that Lord and Judas denote the same person? May we not surmise a connection between the Judas here and the Judas of Josephus? Whence then the change of name from Judas to Jesus? This it will be our business to explain in the subsequent chapters. Meanwhile, remark how very imperfectly this whole subject has been investigated. Take, for instance, the criticism of the relationship which is said to have existed between Jesus and John the Baptist. According to the Gospel accounts, they must have been mutually aware of their relationship to each other. Their respective mothers, the Virgin Mary and Elizabeth, had, it was known, both been visited by the Angel Gabriel, and intimations were supernaturally vouchsafed them of the great future in store for their offspring. It is incredible, after miraculous communications such as these, known, as they were, and recorded by the Apostles, companions of Jesus and John the Baptist, that the knowledge of the fact was concealed from the two principals themselves. Yet Jesus speaks of his cousin John as the greatest of the prophets, and John extols the greatness of Jesus, while both hold such communication with each other as if neither was conscious of any fleshly relationship to the other, and the Apostles themselves seem to forget that they had spoken of any other connection. Yet the circumstances of this relation we have never seen referred to by any of the many critics who have explored this field of inquiry; and this fact is one evidence among a thousand others to warrant the assertion that, after all the criticism which the four Greek writers, as well as the Epistles of Paul, have undergone, nothing of a full and exhaustive nature has yet been attempted, and that when a more accurate analysis is made, conclusions may be forced upon us the reverse of those commonly accepted by the Christian world as orthodox.

It is out of our power, in a work so limited as this, to deal with this great subject as it deserves. To do it full justice would require more learning and literary leisure than has fallen to us. Enough if haply we furnish the key, and then leave to abler hands the unlocking of the historical secrets to which it opens, which have been kept so long hidden behind the veil of mystery, before which men have done worship and built temples as to a God. The leading points we have sought to establish in the course of our argument are these:—That the only religious sect new to Josephus and the Judea of his day was founded by *Judas* of Galilee; that James the Lord's brother was the brother of *Judas;* that *Judas* the Apostle (not Iscariot) is *not* represented as the brother of *Jesus* the *Lord;* that James is not spoken of as the brother of *Jesus, but is called the brother of the Lord and the brother of Judas only.* And we conclude with asking if there is not in all this a presumption that the original name of the Lord of the traditional Gospels was, not Jesus, but Judas? May not the Gospels in this way bear witness to the fact? How the name Judas was changed into Jesus will appear in the chapters that follow.

CHAPTER IX.

The Messianic age — Its rise and fanaticisms — Impostors that appeared — Silence about Jesus — Banus presumably John — The Messiah as yet only an expectation — The martyr-nation.

FEW persons, if any, competent to judge, will question the existence in history of a Messianic age. The first historian who records the fact is Josephus, who was a witness of its existence. It was contemporaneous with his own life and that of his immediate ancestry, and was limited in its manifestation to Judea, the land of his birth; and it is he who has related the incidents which occurred in it, as well as the philosophic views and political agitations, with the errors and crimes, which characterised it. In it the first announcement was made to the world of an expectation, which extended far over the borders of Judea, of the advent of the Messiah in fulfilment of biblical prophecies. It was an age of portents and prodigies, of signs on earth and signs in heaven, and it coincided neither with the period of the procuratorship of Pontius Pilate nor that of the reign of Tiberias. For the insignificant individual who was slain by Pilate, and whose death and that of his followers led to his recall, was neither the founder of a new philosophy nor a pretender to the Messiahship, but simply an impostor. The age referred to commenced when the philosophy of Judas of Galilee began to circulate and find acceptance, partly among the simple-minded, partly among the political zealots and partly among the more restless spirits of the community; and when Caligula at length commanded his image to be set up in Judea and worshipped, then the idea of the kingdom of God as preached by Judas, with its renunciation of all merely human kingship, began violently to seize on the heart and sway the great mass of the people; only as the reign of Caligula was shortlived, and his successor, Claudius Cæsar, commenced his government in a milder and less exacting spirit, the disaffection was for a time allayed and there was no open outburst.

The days of religious fanaticism, however, had set in, and another pretender to prophetical inspiration arose, who endeavoured to delude the people. This was when Fadus was procurator of Judea, in the early days of Claudius Cæsar. This impostor was called Theudas.[*] "He persuaded a great part of the people to take their effects with them and follow him to the river Jordan; for he told them he was a prophet, and that he would, by his own command, divide the river, and afford them an easy passage over it."

Up to this moment no mention whatever is made of *Jesus Christ:* of him, if he existed previously, all his contemporaries are silent, and that though the

[*] Antiquities, Book xx. cap. 5, § 1.

names of many others are given who were pretenders to divine powers, or powers, at least, transcending such as are normal to humanity.

The procuratorship of Felix, which extended to the reign of Nero, witnessed further attempts at innovation under the pretext of a Divine commission.

"The works that were done by the robbers filled the city with all sorts of impiety. And now these impostors and deceivers persuaded the *multitude* to follow them into the wilderness, and pretended that they would exhibit manifest wonders and signs, that should be performed by the providence of God. And many that were prevailed on by them suffered the punishment of their folly; for Felix brought them back and then punished them. Moreover, there came *out of Egypt* about this time to Jerusalem, one that said he was a prophet, and advised the multitude of the *common people* to go with him to the *Mount of Olives*, as it was called, which lay over against the city, and at the distance of five furlongs. He said further that he would show them from hence how, at his command, *the walls of Jerusalem would fall down*, and he promised them that he would procure them an entrance into the city through those walls, when they were fallen down. Now, when Felix was informed of these things, he ordered his soldiers to take their weapons; and came against them with a great number of horsemen and footmen from Jerusalem, and attacked the Egyptian and the people that were with him. He also slew *four hundred of them*, and took two hundred alive. But the Egyptian himself escaped out of the fight, and did not appear any more. And again the robbers stirred up the people to *make war* with the Romans, and said they ought not to obey them at all; and when any person would not comply with them, they set fire to their villages and plundered them."*

Here, again, we have another pretender to divine powers of no great significance portrayed by the historian of the day, and still not one word of Jesus of Nazareth. The case referred to is one more instance of the existence and influence on the popular mind of the religion of Judas of Galilee, and the prevailing expectation of a Messiah, which tended to make men impatient of every other authority, and converted, at length, a community collected together under the name of religion into a gang of open robbers, who pillaged right and left from those who would not consent to go along with them in their revolutionary action. Why, it is natural to ask, are there accounts on the page of history of these inconsiderable fanatics, and no word of Jesus, who is traditionally represented as having so acted and spoken as to have impressed his disciples with the conviction that he was the co-equal of the Deity, the doer of many wonderful works, the founder of a new religion which was to swallow up and sweep away every other; who when alive brought the dead to life and stilled the turbulence of the sea; over whose person the heavens opened, and out of which the astonished human ear heard God's own voice saying, "This is my beloved son, in whom I am well pleased;" one on whom had fallen the mantle of Moses and Elijah, who descended from heaven to pay him homage and resign

* Antiquities, Book xx. cap. 8, § 6.

him their thrones? Of all this the pages of authentic history are silent, and that though the subject thereof is said to have preached his doctrine from mountain-tops to assembled multitudes, and fed his hungry followers by thousands,—not with manna, but with substantial bread and fish miraculously multiplied; and though there were numbers alive who had witnessed his death amid darkness on the cross, been with him after his resurrection from the dead, shared in the enthusiasm which followed his ascension to heaven, and wrought signs and wonders by faith in his name, as the prince of life to the world!

Festus succeeds Felix, and a new impostor appears, but still no word of Jesus.

"So Festus sent forces, both horsemen and footmen, to fall upon those that had been seduced by a certain impostor, *who promised them deliverance and freedom* from the miseries they were under, if they would but follow him as far as the wilderness. Accordingly those forces that were sent destroyed both him that had deluded them and those that were his followers also."*

Pretenders to Messianic powers followed each other at this time in rapid succession, and deluded more or fewer by promises of deliverance by the right hand of God from the miseries the nation suffered under the Roman domination. Many of these pretenders, much as they, with their followers, suffered for their superstitious beliefs and proceedings, were themselves the victims of a delusion that was

* Antiquities, Book xx. cap. 8, § 10.

inspired by others, on whose shoulders, therefore, the responsibility lay. Not till a later period does a pretender of the name of Jesus appear on record; for one of this name comes to light just as the Jewish state is falling to pieces, on the eve of the destruction of the city with its holy Temple. He is preceded by that religious teacher whose reputation for piety, renunciation of all worldly ties and engagements, and insistance on baptismal purification are mentioned by Josephus, who, as we have seen, resided with him for three years, that is, sixteen years subsequent to the recall of Pontius Pilate.

Now, if St. Luke's chronology be accepted, John the Baptist would at this time be about thirty-six years of age; and surely such a character as this could not already be forgotten. Or is it not more probable that *Banus*, with whom Josephus was associated, and whose name, by the way, is derived from a word signifying "*to dip*," is really the identical person spoken of under the name of John in a subsequent age, which learns for the first time, from four Greek writers, yclept apostles, that he, as Baptist, lived at an earlier date precisely such a life as is here indicated historically by Josephus, who, however, is not aware of any other person as leading such an ascetic life? Would Josephus have referred to this Banus as the head of a particular sect of Judaism, and yet be silent about John the Baptist, had a different individual of that name and ascetic life previously existed? Would he not have referred to Banus as the follower or disciple of this John, whom, in the case assumed, he must have succeeded after only a year or two's interval? Would even Banus have become as famous as Josephus represents if he had been born at a later date than that which the chronology of Luke assigns to the birth of John? It would require many years of private training and public manifestation before any one could acquire such historical prominence as is assigned by Josephus to Banus in his autobiography; and we may well conclude, therefore, that the Banus of Josephus is the John of Evangelical tradition.

Considerations such as these tend to fix for us the proper chronology; and the fixing of this is an important point towards the establishment of the truth. The many incidents occurring at different periods both prior and subsequent to the procuratorship of Pilate should be most conscientiously studied by all lovers of historical truth; and history, which even Christianity regards as a most sacred domain, ought not so to be tampered with in the interest of any theology as to shock the sensibilities of all unprejudiced men. And so far is the testimony of history from confirming the dates of the traditional accounts, that we find, as we read the historic page, that we have already finished the reigns of Tiberias, Caligula, and Claudius, and advanced into the reign of Nero before we come upon the name of Jesus. Up to this period there is no mention whatever either of him or his religion, or the wonderful works on which, according to the Evangelists, he grounded his title to respect.

The Mosaic religion was, as we have already seen, divided at this period into four sects, three of which were of more or less ancient date, and the new sect founded about the period of the Cyrenian taxation by Judas of Galilee. This latter sect was an innovation on the old *cultus*, and introduced new forms; it was instinct with superstitious enthusiasm, and blended politics with the sacred rites of religion, having in view the breaking of the Roman yoke and the establishment, pure and simple, of the kingdom of God, whose administration was to be a sacerdotal one in the hands of the high-priest, who should rule the nation according to the laws of God. Towards the realisation of this state of things the Messiah was expected, and pretenders to Messianic power in consequence followed each other in rapid succession, who promised the deliverance sought for to multitudes of dupes. The Roman authorities knew of the prevailing delusion, and treated it as a political subterfuge to effect the overthrow of the Roman yoke. Pontius Pilate's recall from the procuratorship for destroying, along with his followers, the pretended prophet, whom we have so often referred to, was prompted by the conviction that the act was a political blunder, the Samaritan senate having satisfied the imperial authorities that there was no insurrectionary spirit or meaning in the attempt. The Roman world became familiar with the story of these transactions, and the memory of them subsequently blended themselves, more or less transformed, in the traditional accounts that apply to Jesus.

The Roman procurators, however, continued to regard every new pretender to miraculous powers and a supernatural commission with grave misgiving, and they did not scruple to destroy as many of them and their followers as they could convict. Up to this stage, it is to be observed that the delusion did not take the form of a belief that the Messiah *had actually appeared;* the delusion bore only the character of an assured immediate expectation, never the delusion, as afterwards, of men who preached a Messiah who had come, who had died, and who had risen again, but it was the delusion arising from the imposture of men who, to influence the multitude, pretended to Divine inspiration.

No other nation in the world had even in the slightest degree such an expectation; it was confined entirely to the Jewish nation; and it was this belief that a Messiah of the seed of David would appear to reign over the remnant of Judah which was the inspiring idea of all these false pretenders, and which gained acceptance for their deceptive arts. The multitude, all too ready to lend a credulous ear to such pretensions, were slow to believe they had been misled, and only confessed themselves mistaken when the impostor stood self-defeated before the task he had taken up and the problem that, by his assumption of the Messianic office, he had undertaken to work out. The prince of peace, which was the character the Messiah was expected to fulfil, was to conquer and subdue all warfaring and discord, and bring all the tribes of mankind into friendly relationship with one another, under the worship of the one great God, who had hitherto been in covenant only with the Jewish race. Each pretender in succession failed to accomplish this prediction, and one fell after another into ignominious disgrace. But the enthusiasm connected with this expectation did not die out till there was no longer any commonwealth to struggle for, and the Holy City with its Temple was swept from the face of the earth.

The fate thus provoked was not confined to the Jewish nation and the land of Judea; it was the common doom of all lands and nations that dared to resist the all-subduing domination of Rome. The Jewish race would have succumbed at an earlier period but for their obstinate defiance of every insult offered to their stern old faith. No other nation at that period had an idea to fight for, no other a faith such as that conceived by the followers of the Mosaic creed. Other nations might fall before the deified images of Augustus, Tiberias, or Caligula; the Jews never would or could. Hated, despised, and down-trodden they might be, they were the only people who, though they were few in numbers and weak in power, would rather die than accept a merely human domination, even though that should call itself the mistress of all nations, and clothe itself in the terrors of Imperial Rome. The spectacle was a unique one in that era of the world. No nation before or since has shown such faith. They were a *nation* of martyrs.

Only let us note it was the expectation of a Messiah, and *not* the *advent* of one, which brought Palestine to destruction, and the true history of the period confirms this conclusion. It was this expectation that gave the zealots and demagogues such influence over the mass of the people, and checkmated the efforts of a minority to preserve the nation and prevent its dispersion over the surface of the earth.

CHAPTER X.

Appearance of the historical Jesus—His compassion and spirit—His conduct, treatment, and fate—Parallel between this meek Jesus and the Jesus of tradition.

THE procurator of Judea who preceded Gessius Florus, during whose administration the great war broke out, was Albinus. He scrupled not to accept of bribes from the Sicarii, before whose outrages neither life nor property was safe, and to wink at, if not profit by, their iniquitous spoliations. His complicity, however, was not generally known, and it was left to his successor, Gessius Florus, whose actions were as brutal as they were unjust, to arouse the passions and hostility of the people to a pitch which only bloodshed and destruction could quench. There was discontent till then, and much injustice arising from the wicked complicity of Albinus, but no appeal to arms or open revolt. It was a period of portents and prodigies, as authentic history reports. The fate which shortly after befell the Temple, the city, and the people, was not as yet apprehended. The security of the nation was not threatened; comparative peace prevailed, even though it might be interrupted occasionally by those local agitations which must ever disturb a protectorate that connives at public criminality and is indifferent to the common good.

Such was the state of feeling in the commonwealth, when one day, of a sudden, at the Feast of Tabernacles in the Temple, a wild, fearful cry startled and appalled the congregation. It came from a plebeian or peasant, and its peal was heard far and wide by the multitude. It proclaimed the impending desolation of the Temple and the city, and the dispersion of the people. It was such a presage as Holy Writ gives some idea of when a prophet comes forth at the command of God to denounce His anger against a wicked generation, and doom the city they inhabit to the vengeance of His wrath. This fearful cry was not confined to any particular locality or any special feast; it was repeated at every festival, and its shrill notes heard all over the city while the ceremonial lasted. It was a cry by day and by night, saying, "A voice from the east, a voice from the west, a voice from the four winds, a voice against Jerusalem and the holy house, a voice against the bridegrooms and the brides, and a voice against this whole people." *

This prophecy of destruction and desolation was the proclamation of the historical Jesus, *the only Jesus recognised at the time as a prophet of the Lord by the people*, and it foretold what was coming on the city, the Temple, and the nation.

* "Wars of the Jews," Book vi. chap. 5, § 3.

"This was his cry," says Josephus, "as he went about by day and by night in all the lanes of the city. However, certain of the most eminent among the populace had great indignation at this dire cry of his, and took up the man, and gave him a great number of severe stripes; *yet did not he either say* anything for himself, or anything peculiar to those that chastised him, but still went on with the same words which he cried before. Hereupon our *rulers*, supposing, as the case proved to be, that this was a sort of *divine fury in the man*, brought him to the Roman procurator, where he was whipped *till his bones were laid bare; yet did he not make any supplication for himself* nor shed any tears, but turning his voice to the most lamentable tone possible at every stroke of the whip, his answer was, 'Woe, woe to Jerusalem.' And when Albinus (for he was then our procurator) asked him *who he was, and whence he came, and why he uttered such words, he made no manner of reply to what he said*, but still did not leave off his melancholy ditty, till Albinus took him for a madman and dismissed him. Now during all the time that passed before the war began, *this man did not go near any of the citizens, nor was seen by them while he said so*, but he every day uttered these lamentable words, as if it were his premeditated vow, 'Woe, woe to Jerusalem.' *Nor did he give ill words to any of those that beat him every day*, nor good words to those *that gave him food;* but this was his reply to all men, and indeed no other than a melancholy presage of what was to come. This cry of his was the loudest at the festivals, and he continued this ditty *for seven years and five* months, without growing hoarse or being tired therewith, until the very time that he saw his presage in earnest fulfilled in our siege, when it ceased; for, as he was going round upon the wall, he cried out with his utmost force, 'Woe, woe to the city again, and to the people, and to the holy house;' and just as he added at the last, '*Woe, woe to myself also!*' there came a stone out of one of the engines, and smote him, and killed him immediately; and as he was uttering the very same presages, he gave up the ghost."

This was the only Jesus known in Judea, or by the world at large, as having had at the period we speak of the slightest influence as a prophet upon the men of that generation. He was a man of transcendent meekness, cherishing no hatred to those who persecuted him, even though they seemed to thirst for his life. No reproaches even ever passed his lips; one passion only seemed to possess him, and that was to recall his countrymen to their ancient loyalty, by threat of the terrible woe that was coming upon them if they continued in their guilt. The very Temple would not be spared to them, their city was a doomed city, and the Jewish people and race were to endure a terrible curse, such as their own scriptures forewarned them would smite their apostate hearts. This historical Jesus *was fed*, more or less, by the people, for which he *gave no thanks, nor did he give ill words to any of those that beat him every day.*

This is the Jesus who prophesied the destruction of Jerusalem, the Temple, and the people, in accents enough to appal the most callous, with an earnestness and persistency of denunciation that is unparalleled in the annals of the world. He was brought before the Sanhedrim or Jewish authorities, at whose instance he received a great number of stripes; yet did not he either say anything for himself or anything peculiar "to those that chastised him." It was after inflicting this punishment that the rulers (the Sanhedrim), supposing, as proved to be the case, that there was a sort of *divine fury in the man*, brought him to the Roman procurator, *yet did he not make any supplication for himself*. He was not killed, *but his bones were laid bare;* and he was in such a plight that he was not for some time thereafter anywhere to be seen; for, now, says Josephus, "during all the time that passed before the war began, this man did not go near any of the citizens nor was seen by them."

This is the historical Jesus, whose bones were laid bare, and is so described, with many traditional traits besides, at a later period. It was not unreasonable to surmise, *as he disappeared after this torture*, that he was dead, and so his reappearance might naturally come to be spoken of as a resurrection. His disappearance would give a strong colouring to such a surmise, for he left Jerusalem and disappeared for a time from that section of the Jewish world. "*He rambled about the country, visiting* every city, and in his fits of transport uttered the same terrible prediction, straining his voice to the utmost pitch, yet not enfeebling it. When the war broke out, he went on with the same enthusiasm proclaiming vengeance, *and with crowds of his countrymen returned to Jerusalem.*" * When the siege began, he fixed his

* Bossuet's "Discourses on Universal History."

eyes on the walls, exclaiming with vehemence, "Woe to the city, woe to the Temple, woe to the people;" and as he added at last, "Woe to myself," a stone from a battering engine struck him, and he fell dead on the spot.

This is the meek Jesus who was scourged for witnessing to the *truth* that the judgments of God were abroad and would fall on the devoted city. *His bones were laid bare*, and yet he cursed not his persecutors. He returned to Jerusalem to die, for he knew his time had come. Not unnaturally might he be dissuaded by his followers from returning to Jerusalem, in the apprehension lest he should suffer the same harsh and cruel treatment, or worse, at the hands of the authorities. He knew, however, that he was to die in Jerusalem, and though we do not know it as a historical fact that he predicted his death before he started, it was reasonable to conclude that, as he foresaw his fate, he foretold it. His early history is unknown; he came like a meteor before the Judean world; he suffered stripes, contumely, and death for uttering the truth. Nor did he act alone; he had many followers, and he preached his doctrine from city to city. It was a doctrine of woe, and most unwelcome; and it was delivered during a period of *portents, prodigies, and heavenly signs*, which might well impart a miraculous colouring to otherwise merely natural events, connected with all that befell the city and Temple, and that characterised the period. Authentic history corroborates these statements, but is dead against the assumption that such events took place during the governorship of Pontius Pilate.

The followers of this Jesus may have suffered from the cruelty of Nero. Anyhow events had happened enough to stir up in them emotions of frenzied enthusiasm. They had seen a meek prophet, whose wise warnings had spread far and wide, and had proved himself a tender-hearted lover of his race, fall a victim to the obstinacy of the rulers. Such was the general esteem in which he was held, that he was accounted to have a *divine spirit within him*—a possession which is designated by the historian as a "*divine fury*," language which expresses the same as the popular idea. He had no learning, but he spoke the words of truth. He attained the maturity of manhood before his prophetic powers were recognised and his name became celebrated. His career was a short one, but in the course of it he uttered truths which remain unchallenged to this very day. He preached in the Temple his doomsday philosophy at every feast, and he ranged over all Judea with his warning word, so that the entire nation might know what would befall the Temple, the city, and the people of Judea. So deep-piercing and far-reaching were the tones of his voice, that every man, woman, and child, over the length and breadth of the land, were familiar with them, and the contemporaneous awe-inspiring wonders and signs not unnaturally became associated with himself and his utterances. The miraculous events or phenomena which are recorded by the historian of the day had a most portentous character. In the traditional accounts furnished to the world at a subsequent period by the four Greek narrators of these events, these prodigies first became elaborated into a system of signs and wonders in attestation of his supernatural greatness. If what is unnatural be deemed *miraculous*, then these matters we are about to relate were miracles. We prefer, however, recording them in the language of the historian himself.*

"But before Cæsar had determined anything about these people, or given the commanders any orders relating to them, the soldiers were in such a rage that they set the cloisters on fire, by which means it came to pass that some of these were destroyed by throwing themselves down headlong, and some were burnt in the cloisters themselves. Nor did any one of these escape with his life. *A false prophet* was the occasion of these people's destruction, who had made a public proclamation in the city that very day that 'God commanded them to get up upon the Temple, and that there they should receive miraculous signs of their deliverance.' Now there was then a great number of false prophets suborned by the tyrants to impose upon the people, who denounced this to them, that they should wait for *deliverance from God;* and this was in order to keep them from deserting, and that they might be buoyed up above fear and care by such hopes. Now, a man that is in adversity does easily comply with such promises ; for, when such a seducer makes him believe that he shall be delivered from those miseries which oppress him,

---

* "Wars of the Jews," Book vi. chap. 5, § 2.

then it is that the patient is full of hopes of such deliverance.

"Thus were the miserable people persuaded by these deceivers, and such as belied God himself, while they did not attend nor give credit *to the signs* that were so evident, and did so plainly foretell their future desolation, but, like men infatuated, without either eyes to see or minds to consider, did not regard the denunciations that God made to them. Thus there was a star resembling a sword, *which stood over the city,* and a comet that continued a whole year. Thus also before the Jews' rebellion, and before those commotions which preceded the war, when the people were come in great crowds to the feast of unleavened bread, on the eighth day of the month Xanthicus (Nisan), and at the ninth hour of the night, *so great a light shone* round the altar and the holy house that it appeared to be bright daytime, which light lasted for half an hour. This light seemed to be a good sign to the unskilful, *but was so interpreted by the sacred scribes as to portend those events that followed immediately upon it.* At the same festival (Passover) also, *a heifer, as she was led by the high-priest to be sacrificed, brought forth a lamb in the midst of the Temple.*"

Who that will but study the particulars of this narrative in detail, and that compares them with the story of the Evangelists, can fail to see in the parallel the source of their ideal representation, the chamber of imagery from which they drew the separate features of their fanciful delineation? *Here, at the Passover, we have the idea of the conception suggested by the miraculous birth of a lamb brought forth in the stables of the Temple, to be sacrificed for the sins of* the people; and above in the heavens is shining the curious star which stood over the house where the miraculously conceived being was born.

And lest any one who prefers the testimony of an Apostle to that of Josephus should demur to this account as matter of history, we may be allowed to refer to the evidence of Peter himself. For though it may be that the light described as having shone around the altar and the holy house was only the *aurora borealis*, how comes it that Simon Peter should be believed to have seen *such a light when he escapes from* prison immediately after the sacrifice of this lamb? For Josephus in his description proceeds to describe this very event :—

"Moreover the eastern gate of the inner (court of the) Temple, which was of brass, and vastly heavy, and had been with difficulty shut by twenty men, and rested upon a basis armed with iron, and had bolts fastened very deep into the firm floor, which was there made of one entire stone, was seen to be opened of its own accord, about the sixth hour of the night. Now those that kept watch in the Temple came thereupon running to the captain of the Temple, and told him of it; who then came up thither, and not without great difficulty was able to shut the gate again. This also appeared to the vulgar to be a very happy prodigy, as if God did thereby open to them the gate of happiness. But the men of learning understood it, that the security of their holy house was dissolved of its own accord, and that the gate was opened for the advantage of their enemies; so these *publicly declared* that this signal foreshadowed the desolation that was coming upon them."

No such incidents as these occurred in the time of Pontius Pilate, but there is the historical proof to show that they happened at the period to which we refer, and the Temple records which attest them are unimpeachable. The evidence that will be furnished cannot fail to satisfy those who have any sense of historical truth that this is the so-called Messianic age, and that, as predicted, the people who lived in it did not believe in the true prophet, but the false, till the judgment came upon them, and the words of "the meek and lowly one" were fulfilled. The prophets of the day, who were all false save this one, taught the people to believe that the latter days had come, and that when the worst came to the worst God would interfere and work deliverance.

Jesus had come and gone, and left disciples behind him, who believed that he had a *divine mission* to fulfil and a divine spirit within him. In his decease they both saw the fulfilment of that part of his prophecy which concerned himself and a token, of which there were other infallible indications, that the ruin threatened would not fail to overtake the city and its people also. But before that event arrived, one other miracle took place, of which there are two accounts, one by the historian of the day, and the other in the Acts of the Apostles. The version given by Josephus is as follows: *—"Moreover, at that feast which we call Pentecost, as the priests were going by night into the inner (court of the) Temple,

---

* "Wars of the Jews," Book vi. chap. 5, § 3.

as *their custom was,* to perform their sacred ministrations, they said that in the first place *they felt a quaking and heard a great noise,* and after that they heard a sound, as of a multitude, saying, ' Let us remove hence.'" The version in the Acts in chap. ii. 1, 2 :—" And when the day of Pentecost was fully come, *they were all with one accord in one place.* And suddenly there came a sound from heaven, as of a rushing mighty wind, and it filled the house where they were sitting."

Besides the proofs which we intend to furnish, in order to satisfy the candid reader, there are certain considerations only remotely related to the point in immediate debate which go to show that the historical relation of these transactions and events is the only reliable one, and that the subsequent accounts of the Evangelists are little else than fanatical fancies, that fashioned themselves together in the vague atmosphere of traditional report. Nevertheless, the story they tell, though traditionally conveyed, is historically grounded, and it has been our business all along to show that it is no mere cunningly devised fable. The traditional accounts are supported by the historical in their assertion of miraculous occurrences in connection with the fall of the Jewish state. Both introduce a prophet of the name of Jesus, who foretold the ruin of the nation and perished in the wreck. Both represent him as of humble birth, of meek, patient temper, hardly treated, sorely baffled, and sad at heart. Both, as they had many foes to whom they bore no rancour, so had they many followers to whom they owed no thanks. Both were instinct with a divine spirit, and wandered over Judea, denouncing the judgments of Heaven on all who would not repent. Neither left written record, only the weird echo of their winged piercing words, "Woe! Woe!" Both, strong in the divine justice of their mission, refused to plead for mercy before a human tribunal, and were dumb, opening not the mouth. Both predicted their own decease at Jerusalem, and the bones of both were laid bare in the torture they underwent. Both were looked upon as insane by an unsympathising world, while by a few they were reverenced as God-inspired and prophets of the Lord.

It is notable that the charge of insanity preferred against the Jesus of the Gospels is recorded in the Gospels themselves. Thus in John x. 19, 20, we read:—"There was a division, therefore, among the Jews for these sayings. And many of them said, He hath a devil and is mad; why hear ye him?" In Mark iii. 13-21 we read:—

"And he goeth up into a mountain, and calleth unto him whom he would; and they came unto him. And he ordained twelve, that they should be with him, and that he might send them forth to preach, and to have power to heal sicknesses and to cast out devils. And Simon he surnamed Peter; and James the son of Zebedee, and John the brother of James (and he surnamed them Boanerges, which is, The sons of thunder); and Andrew, and Philip, and Bartholomew, and Matthew, and Thomas, and James the son of Alpheus, and Thaddeus, and Simon the Canaanite, and Judas Iscariot, which also betrayed him : and they went into an house. And the multitude cometh together again, so that they could not so much as eat bread. *And when his friends heard of it, they went out to lay hold on him; for they said, He is beside himself.*"

And in vers. 31–34, at the same time and place, it is further recorded :—

"There came then his brethren and his mother, and standing without, sent unto him, calling him. And the multitude sat about him; and they said unto him, Behold thy mother and thy brethren without seek for thee. And he answered them, saying, Who is my mother or my brethren? And he looked round about on them which sat about him, and said, Behold my mother and my brethren!"

Thus we see, according to the Evangelical record itself, this charge is preferred against Christ, in the presence of his disciples, by his own relations, and among the number the very mother that bore him, since worshipped by so many as the mother of God. We see her there thrusting herself forward amid the listening crowds that surrounded him, and, with the rest of his friends and relatives, attempting to lay hands on him as "beside himself,"—that mother to whom the Angel Gabriel had foretold that he would sit on the throne of David his father, who had seen him turn water into wine at the marriage in Cana of Galilee, and had witnessed him make the dumb speak, the deaf hear, the blind see, and the dead live,—it is she we see making this charge against him, in the presence of his Apostles too, and before a multitude who are hanging upon his lips, and with whom, in her mother's heart, she could not but wish he should stand well. *See*, do we say? Who can conceive such a scene as this? who, above all, with such a faith as the Church has in the mother and the son?—the mother, since regarded by millions as almost equal to her son, ranked, by virtual denial of her son's divinity here, by this act of unbelief, among the number of the lost; and the son, who could forgive the malice of his adversaries, because he knew their ignorance, spurning an anxiety, which he could not but know sprung from the soft yearning affection of a mother's love?

For if she believed not in him, she at least loved him; hence her attempt, with the assistance of his brethren, to lay hands on him, all the more that they said, "*He is beside himself.*" It is in this feature of the picture the truth comes out: the mother's feeling waxes transcendent, and she would go forth to take him home to her, and nurse him as in his youth. Perhaps it was he had no food or shelter, and she would give him both; and he himself was wont to say, "Foxes have holes, and the birds of the air have nests, but the Son of man hath not where to lay his head." So that it appears the Jesus of the Gospels as well as the Jesus of history depended upon others for the relief of his daily necessities. Anyhow, here are two traits in which the traditional and the historical Jesus correspond: both exposed themselves to the charge of insanity, and both exposed themselves to this reproach by a most singular life.

So long as the Evangelists are historically faithful, so long is their story credible; but as soon as they leave the region of fact for that of philosophy, they lose their senses and give birth to the sheerest absurdities. What can be more monstrous, for instance, than the picture we have here, as elsewhere, of the son as contrasted with the mother? He is God of very God, and yet he cannot persuade his mother—who withal is so prepared and predisposed to believe in him, that he is what he says—that he is other than "beside himself." He certainly could have removed his mother's unbelief, had he been God; and had he been a good man, he would not have pretended to divine power. It is, therefore, inconceivable how he could have been Son of God, when he lacked the power of divinity, and was deficient in the affection of ordinary humanity. The conception of being Son of Mary and Son of God is an impossible one, and the attempt to embody it can only issue in defeat. And in this case the human ideal suffers as much as that of divinity; the representation is as faulty in the former reference as the latter. The dutifulness of Jesus as a son is as questionable as the power claimed for him as deity; nay, there is a scene towards the close of his life where he utters words that make him appear deficient in a higher piety still. In Mark vi. 4. we read as follows :—

"But Jesus said unto them, A prophet is not without honour, but in his own country, and among his own kin, and in his own house."

And again in Matthew xxvii. 46 :—

"And about the ninth hour Jesus cried with a loud voice, saying, Eli, Eli, Lama Sabachthani? that is to say, My God, my God, why hast Thou forsaken me?"

Here we find the only begotten Son of God reproaching his earthly mother for her unbelief, and crying out against the desertion of his heavenly Father, although it is alleged that he covenanted with that Father to give up his life for humanity.

Let us conclude this chapter by recalling the reader's attention to the parallel we have sought to draw between the Jesus of Josephus and the Jesus of the Gospels. Is it not surprising that Josephus should make no mention of the first Jesus, who suffered under Pontius Pilate, and the Evangelists no mention of the second Jesus, so like the first in spirit and fate, and who suffered during the siege of the Holy City? Can any other explanation account for this singular circumstance and the singular correspondence in the characters and history of the two prophets, except that, with all their inconsistencies otherwise, the accounts refer to the same period, the same incidents, and the same Jesus?

CHAPTER XI.

Messianic delusions and their consequences—Mistakes about the last days—Christian idolatry, and the woes it has caused—Reconciliation proposed—The real Jesus and the false prophets.

So far, then, it is evident beyond all cavil that, had the Jews listened to the warnings of the historical Jesus, their Temple, their city, and their commonwealth would have been preserved. Titus did not seek their destruction; only such continued obedience and payment of tribute as was due for protection, and such homage as other nations yielded to the power and supremacy of Rome. It was his ardent wish to spare the Temple, the ancient city, and its people from destruction; and he again and again signified to the besieged this wish. He even employed the mediation of Josephus himself, and literally implored them to yield, if they would be spared. These stern realities are worthy of weighty consideration; they show that great delusions are founded upon great facts; that it is not in human beings to build altogether upon myths and legends, though they often enough so exaggerate truth as to resolve it into fiction. This weakness of humanity is of daily exhibition, and turns up in a thousand ways, now swaying the imagination of the vulgar, now that of the educated and more refined. The undeniable fact, however, has been put plainly before the Jewish world, and cannot be gainsaid, that the prophecies of the historical Jesus have been realised to the letter; that their Temple, their city, and their nation were ruined because they refused to listen to his denunciations; and that it was their adoption of the Messianic idea from the false prophets of the day that determined them to resist to the bitter end, in consequence of which they were almost annihilated, and that they bequeathed to the remnant of the people an unexampled persecution of "Woe, woe, from the four winds," from the four quarters of the globe, which has lasted now for eighteen hundred years.

The fulfilment of this prophecy is peculiarly remarkable, and deserves grave reflection. It was fulfilled by an unseen agency. Titus evinced the most intense desire to save the Temple and the city, and certainly the Jews themselves were not less eager to escape destruction. How did it come to pass, then, seeing besieged and besieger equally deprecated the fulfilment of Jesus's prophecy, that it was fulfilled in spite of both their wishes, and in spite of the warning which, had they listened to it, would have saved the city? The way in which the prophecy was to be fulfilled was foretold in the words in which the judgment was denounced: "Woe, woe, to the people from the four winds," *from the four quarters of the globe.*

The Jewish race were, according to this prophecy, to suffer relentless enmity and persecution at the hands of the whole world, and the prophecy was uttered at a time when they were not even at war with the Romans, and no human eye could have foreseen that for nearly eighteen centuries this people would be tossed about by the four winds of heaven, a prey to the anger of Him whom yet in their hearts they revered.

As far as human insight can discern, it would seem that the sufferings of the Jewish race have been occasioned by their rejection of the warnings of the historical Jesus, *and by their blind faith in those false prophets* who persuaded them to hope in a promised deliverance at the hands of one from the seed of David, who would appear and save them in their hour of sorest need. Only, while this was their hope, it is certain there was no idolatry in such an expectation. Such an one, whether false or true, would never be revered as a divinity; he would be venerated at most as a high-priest of the Deity, for with the Jew none is or ever can be accounted equal in majesty and sublimity to the Most High and Creator of the world.

The creed of the Christian is, on the other hand, an idolatrous creed, and is utterly alien to the Jewish faith. The Messiah of the Christian has, in the regard of the Jew, usurped the glory and worship of the Almighty; and it is of the essence of Christianity to identify Jesus with God. This doctrine was indeed first taught by Jews; they were the first delinquents, and it is for the propagation of this great delusion that the Jewish race still suffers at the hands of God. But for the guilt of introducing the creed of Christianity into the world, that race would not have undergone the long trial of sorrow with which it has been afflicted in the centuries which have passed since the perpetration of the crime. It is equally clear and historically established that the *Christian Messianic period was a huge delusion,* and not all the sophistry and Jesuitry of the world will erelong be able to hide from the advancing intelligence of the age the knowledge of this portentous fact. Where is the man competent to judge who dare affirm that the Messianic theories of the four Greek writers have not been contradicted in their most vital parts by time and experience? Both those who looked for a Messiah to come and those who look for a Messiah to return, have been disappointed. The last days according to both have come, and he has not, as both predicted, appeared to deliver. Not all the sophistry in the world can, at this stage of the world's history, delude its inhabitants any longer on these points.

These are *ascertained delusions,* and can no longer be maintained by an ingenuous mind. Time and experience have utterly dissipated them. They were once and for long received with a veneration equal to that still extended by the Christian world to the other revelations of the Christian faith; but now it can no longer be pretended that the last days promised in connection with the Messiah's appearance or return have come or are coming, that the hope of the false prophets or the faith of the Christians has in *that* regard been fulfilled. The promise of return, with which Christ comforted his disciples when he left them, has failed, and therewith must go confidence in him as a true prophet.

The Greek Gospels were written to the world in unambiguous language, that God had visited the earth and announced Himself as the redeemer and lord of the human family. Their declaration notified to the world that Jesus was both Christ and God; that the latter days had come; that, after his ascension to heaven, he would return in the clouds before that generation had passed away; and that some of those to whom this promise was given should be still alive when the Son of man came back again in all his glory. Thus do these four Greek writers, by ascribing to God pledges which He has not redeemed, lay to His charge falsehoods, and involve themselves in a crime which, were it perpetrated now, would be called the height of impiety. But what is ancient is venerated, whether false or true; nay, the antiquity sometimes screens the perpetrators from detection; but in this case there is no loophole of escape. Neither metaphysics nor theology, neither the theory of types or accommodations nor historical fact, can assist these authors out of the dilemma in which they have involved themselves in the most important particulars connected with their revelation. These writings affirm that the *latter days* are come, and the Messiah with them, in *conformity with* Old Testament prophecies. The Christian critic now partly admits that the latter days have not come, but he refuses to admit that the advent of his Messiah has not taken place, although the Messiah himself expressly asserted that the latter days were nigh, that they would appear in that generation, and that before that generation expired, he would appear in the clouds of heaven surrounded by his angels.

How men of truth and honour, such as abound in Christendom, can accept as divine declarations such contradictory assertions is past all comprehension. It utterly baffles us to understand how they can reconcile frauds and impostures such as these with their notions of deity, and how they can fancy him to be divine who has so deceived the nations. The truth is :—The whole is a Jewish delusion from first to last ; and Jew and Christian must confer together on the point, and consent to mutual explanations and exculpations. We, as the remnant of the race that first offended, must ask forgiveness from our Christian brethren whom our fathers misled, and they must grant us absolution on the ground that our race has suffered so much from their perversity and that of their ancestors. The woes from fire and sword, the woes from scorn and oppression, the woes from an enslaved mind and conscience, the woes from the Inquisition, the woes from banishment, the woes from an attempted extermination, and the woes from an enforced idolatrous worship,—all these evils were deserved by our race for the false teaching it has imparted to the

Christian world. And then we have inflicted a greater evil than we ourselves have suffered, for we have infected others with an idolatrous worship, which we think worse than death, to the teaching of which *alone* we can historically trace all the evils which have followed us as a people from the destruction of our city and the dispersion of our tribes down to the present day. Let us then try to undo the great evil we have perpetrated; let us in singleness of heart ask our brethren of the present generation, who have so signally disapproved of the actions of their forefathers by refusing to imitate them, to forgive our trespasses against them as we forgive their trespasses against us. Let us in candour of spirit and brotherly love take up the fallacies one by one and expose them, not in scorn or bitterness of spirit, but with the simple endeavour to undo what we have done, and so repair the evil which has emanated from our race.

It is the Jewish historian of the so-called Messianic period who testifies that prophets belonging to that period, and affecting a divine commission, were a curse to the men of his generation; that their declarations were false; that they excited multitudes to believe in their pretensions; that they stirred up a wild enthusiasm among the people, which he deliberately designates a madness; and that the infection deepened and spread till it precipitated the Jewish race and their glorious Temple, which was the wonder of the world, into a common abyss of destruction. The same historian attests that this madness was not the inspiration of Jesus, but that it came from Judas of Galilee and a *new sect of which he was the founder;* that the historical Jesus, who appeared later on, strove with prophetic earnestness to rectify this false teaching, by assuring his contemporaries that by adopting it they not only threatened with destruction their Temple and their city, but were letting loose upon the nation the four winds of heaven, to scatter it far and wide over the surface of the earth. There was nothing ambiguous in his denunciation; it was a fulmination against the delusion which emanated from Judas of Galilee, and had spread among the people under the teaching of his sect; and this is a fact which, in the interests of mankind, we may challenge any one to contradict.

The admission of this may constitute a new platform for both Jews and Christians; not a platform based, as hitherto, upon myths and legends, but upon the firm ground of historical truth. It may not be received at first with favour either by the one sect or the other, but what cannot be truthfully combated must and will eventually prevail. If the Jews deny the traditional accounts of Jesus, they will not dispute what can be proved to be historically true concerning him, even though that may compel them to admit the fulfilment of prophecies that tell against themselves. If they have hitherto failed to acknowledge any feature in the character or any fact in the life of Jesus, it has arisen from the exaggeration of the traditional writers who introduced him to the world so many years after his death, and whose accounts, from their palpable untruth, are unworthy of credence. They have in their fancy clothed him with so many disguising attributes that he is become unrecognisable among the figures of the historical world, appearing in their accounts only as a deified portrait by the hands of a number of artists, who have depicted his likeness from memory after his death. Nearly every feature has been distorted in the atmosphere of tradition under the enthusiasm of intense religious belief. If the accounts given by the four Greek writers of Jesus, of his wonderful character and his eventful momentous history, had been true, the relation of these would not have depended upon traditional statements. It had been a miracle indeed had such astounding transactions of Heaven on earth remained without record for so many years, when historians, both Jewish and others, were alive at the time, who made it their very business to record the public events of the period, and that so minutely as to hand down to posterity the most graphic details respecting, not only the religious and social features that characterised it, but even the signs observed in the heavens and regarded as ominous of coming changes. Indeed, the history of the period we refer to, which makes no allusion to Jesus, his religion, or the miracles attending him, constitutes *a denial of the Pontius Pilate era of miracles which no subsequent accounts can ever destroy.*

That Jesus did not, as the traditional accounts allege, suffer during the era of Pontius Pilate, but, as the historical relation shows, at a later period, is borne out by the chronology of St. Luke. St. Luke tells us that Jesus was born at the period of the Cyrenian taxation, which would make him only twenty when he was crucified; while John, on the other hand, chap. viii. 56, 57, quoting what Jesus had said:—"Your father Abraham rejoiced to see my day, and he saw it, and was glad," makes those who heard him exclaim, "Thou art not yet fifty years old, and hast thou seen Abraham?" It would be wholly unfitting for the Jews to say to a mere youth, a stripling of nineteen or twenty years old, "Thou art not yet fifty years old;" and it is St. Luke who is our authority for saying he *was* a mere youth at that period. Anyhow, here we have St. Luke bearing out the assertion that Jesus was not the person who suffered under Pontius Pilate, and confirming the statement made by Josephus, that it was another who then pretended to prophecy, and whose fate brought the procurator himself into disgrace and trouble. Thus does St. Luke confirm the testimony of Josephus, who both mentions the case of the pretender that suffered at the hands of Pilate and describes the Jesus who appeared on the eve of the destruction of the city, and sealed with his blood his protest against the mad Messianic furor of the time, which was bringing down on his devoted country the judgment of Heaven. Thus is Josephus historically just, while the four Greek writers are historically unjust, for they only refer to one prophet, ascribing the characteristics and the name of Jesus to the first pretender, while they are altogether silent about the very existence of Josephus' Jesus. The discrepancy between the two accounts is almost confined to difference of period, but this difference can by the most striking proofs be clearly shown to be *the error of the four Greek writers*, and *not* the error of Josephus. By heavenly phenomena and earthly, by the declarations of St. Luke, by the declarations of St. Peter, by the declaration of the Acts of the Apostles, and by the utterance of Jesus himself, it is undeniably established that the traditional Jesus was really and truly no other than this historical Jesus; and the proof of the identification will be rendered more complete as we adduce additional coincidences in the chapters that follow.

CHAPTER XII.

The dual character of Jesus, whence—The chronology set right—Promise in regard to the last days unfulfilled—How the traditional Jesus developed out of the historical—Inconsistencies in the character and teaching referable to two personalities.

An ordinary reader of the Gospels cannot fail to remark the dual character they ascribe to Jesus; it is so clearly taught by them that he has two natures, and those natures very incompatible with each other. His idiosyncrasies had, it appears, developed the belief of this singular duality, while the image presented is of only one Jesus. It is asserted that he has two natures, if only one body; and in consequence the Christian Church has, without tracing its origin, adopted this view of his personality as a chief article of its creed. It will be our business to explain the origin of this conception, and prove by historical evidence that the two natures are referable originally to *two different persons,* both of whom bore the name Jesus, lived at the same time, and had each a very marked character—men whose deeds, whose sentiments, whose characteristics, whose friends and colleagues and their characteristics, together with the incidents that befell them, compose when combined the main features of the picture drawn by the four Greek writers, which is our traditional embodiment of the historical facts. The children of those who were witnesses of the facts did not entirely misinform those who gathered their statements and put them in form, and the error in the chronology, which ascribes the main event to the era of Pontius Pilate, is easily accounted for by reference to the historical fact that a pretender to prophecy had been executed by that procurator, in a way to afford presumptive evidence that those who got up the story had no actual intention to falsify the facts. We therefore exempt those who supplied the traditional accounts from the serious charge of fraud, which we are forced to prefer against the compilers of a later period, where the perversions which sprung out of the tradition itself were fraudulently and unjustly used as reliable evidence in proof of the truth of gross errors.

We have already quoted the testimony of Josephus to the existence of the prophetic Jesus, whose intense character and emphatic procedure suggested the idea of a man possessed by a *divine fury*. This historical description, translated into the Greek language by the author himself, could not fail to confirm and intensify the statement made by tradition, that Jesus of Nazareth was a *divine character*. No other historical character is so described, and the wonderful fulfilment of his prophecies in his own death and the general desolation of Judea and destruction of the Temple, might well furnish the groundwork for those representations of events which, as inexplicable by any known law of cause and effect, are regarded as supernatural and miraculous to this day. It is true that though they are described as presages, portents, and prodigies, they would at this time of day come under the head of what are termed phenomena; but be this as it may, we can see strong reasons for believing that they were deemed miracles; and indeed, under the circumstances, many of the incidents so described are sufficiently inexplicable to exonerate those who so regarded them from the charge of wilful fraud in appealing to them in proof; while we must not forget that the accounts committed to writing were traditions collected, probably, from a multitude of different sources, each supplying a trait differing one from another, without exact dates, and each bringing into one moment incidents that took place on different occasions, many of them true, and confirmed by contemporary historians. These accounts are given without regard to *that division of time* which can only be arrived at, as a rule, after the most accurate inquiry, and which is sure to fall awry in mere traditional reports, which cannot be relied upon after a single year's transmission, still less from generation to generation.

If a historian erroneously records incidents which took place in the lifetime of thousands of his contemporaries, he is certain to be apprised by some of them of the errors he has committed, and if, in spite of correction, he wilfully stands fast to his accounts, he cannot escape the reproach of being an untruthful historian; but if, on the contrary, he is most accurate in his assertions, as well as just in his judgments, he will be appreciated by all his own contemporaries, and more particularly by those of them who were living witnesses of what he describes. Now Josephus describes the Pontius Pilate era, and mentions the deceiver who met his death at that Governor's hands. The deceits practised by him were ascertained deceits, his delusions were ascertained delusions. He did nothing of a miraculous character; and though he promised to show on the top of Mount Gerizim many wonderful things "placed there by Moses," it was ascertained that his statement was false, and that he deceived those who trusted him. Josephus it is, who earned his reputation for accuracy when the witnesses to the facts narrated were still alive, that gives the account we have so often referred to of the Pontius Pilate pretender, and it is he too that furnishes the account of the *Jesus* whom we have designated as the historical Jesus, and that in his description speaks of his appearance as a presage of woe to Jerusalem, to the people, and to the Temple.

Now how is it that he should describe this latter personage as a prophet of truth, and the Pontius Pilate victim as a lying pretender? Why should he represent this Jesus as prophesying, in the most public manner, in the Temple and out of it, the judgment of God against the city and the race, and yet speak of the other as only a common deceiver?

Would he have enumerated the prophetic qualifications possessed by *Jesus*, and yet shrunk from mentioning those of the Pontius Pilate pretender, if he possessed them? If he hesitated to ascribe preternatural attributes to the Pontius Pilate pretender, he would have equally hesitated to do so to the historical Jesus. But Josephus *dared* not, even if he had been disposed, ascribe, in the teeth of living witnesses, to the Pontius Pilate pretender those prophetical utterances which emanated from Jesus, a contemporary of his own day, who was too marked and well-known a character to be capable of distortion or perversion. If the Pontius Pilate pretender had been called Jesus, if he had prophesied the destruction of Jerusalem and its Temple, as well as his own death, if indeed he had performed one hundredth part of the wonders related by the four Greek writers of Christ, how could it have been possible for the historian to have omitted or disguised the fact, and that in the presence of those who believed in him as the Messiah of the latter days, and looked for his return while they were yet alive in the flesh?

The Gospel narrative discloses the fact that Jesus promised to return to the earth immediately after the tribulation of those days, and the desolation predicted by Daniel. The 24th chapter of Matthew affords ample proof of this assertion, and we must quote in corroboration a verse or two (chap. xxiv. 13-31):—

"But he that shall endure unto the end, the same shall be saved. And this gospel of the kingdom shall be preached in all the world for a witness unto all nations, and then shall the end come. When ye therefore shall see the abomination of desolation spoken of by Daniel the prophet stand in the *holy place* (whoso readeth let him understand), then let them which be in Judea flee into the mountains: let him which is on the housetop not come down to take anything out of his house: neither let him which is in the field return back to take his clothes. And *woe* unto them that are with child, and to them which give suck in those days. But pray ye that your flight be not in the winter, neither on the sabbath-day. For then shall be great tribulation, such as was *not since the beginning of the world* to this time, no, nor *ever shall be. . . . Immediately after the tribulation of those days* shall the sun be darkened, and the moon shall not give her light, and the stars shall fall from heaven, and the powers of the heavens shall be shaken. And then shall appear the sign of the Son of man in heaven; and then shall all the tribes of the earth mourn; and they shall see the Son of man coming in the clouds of heaven with power and great glory. And he shall send his angels with a great sound of a trumpet, and they shall gather together his elect *from the four winds*, from one end of heaven to the other."

These quotations serve a double purpose: they convict, in the first place, this Gospel of testifying unto all nations of its own *falsity*, for the end has not come, although eighteen hundred years have elapsed since the abomination of desolation spoken of by Daniel the prophet stood in the holy place; and we may well add the concluding part of the 15th verse quoted, "*Whoso readeth let him understand.*" Time and experience, as we again urge, have proved to all nations the utter untruthfulness of these writings in this most important point, albeit the most preferring *expediency* to truth, the fewest are prepared to accept the conclusion to which the fact leads; they will hold out as long as possible, because they feel themselves bound to defend the faith which they have inherited from their fathers, and because mayhap the teachings, however idolatrous they may be, certainly have blended with them grand moral lessons, which many fear may become uncertain if the idolatry and the revolting theology involved in it should be given up. That the abominable idolatries of this creed have been tolerated and retained, is due we believe in great part to the sublime morality with which it is interblended, and which it must be allowed by all is the one vital centre and germ of the Christian faith. The time is not far distant, however, when the falsehood mixed up in it will be purged from its substance, and then let us hope the pure gold that is in it will shine forth with a lustre which it has never shed before.

Apart from these reflections, however, it does not appear illogical that the four Greek writers should have believed what tradition reported to them; still, as the narrative, collected from various sources, was committed to writing long after the fall of Jerusalem, we may not unreasonably inquire why they do not refer to the historical Jesus of that date, all the more that the traditional Jesus was expected to reappear,

and that publicly, at or a little later than the period
in which he lived and came to the front. The only
explanation of this is to be found in the fact that the
tradition handed down to the four Greek writers as a
tradition referred to this very Jesus of whom Josephus
relates. Years had elapsed since the appearance of
this remarkable personage, and his career and fate
could not fail to leave a deep impression on the
generation that followed. His denunciations must
have revived in a weird light in the hearts of men
after their actual realisation, and must have stamped
themselves on the memory as the words of a prophet
of the Lord; and his character as the possessor of
divine attributes would, with each succeeding generation, gradually assume a more and more definite shape
as a divine incarnation, the whole being in all probability a development of our historian's characterisa-
tion of him as a man aflame with a divine fury, and of
his description of him as he sent forth his wail of woe
on the highway and at the solemn feasts. His heroic
appearance under sentence of the rulers of the people
and the Governor, when, though his bones were
laid bare, he gave utterance to no repining, could not
fail to enhance the idea of him in the hearts of his worshippers, and give plausibility, along with other manifestations, to their conception of him as a god. And
all the more would this conception of him tend to
assume this shape when it was remembered that he
uttered his dire denunciations concerning Jerusalem,
which were so tragically fulfilled, at a time when the

horizon seemed clear of storms, and no mere human eye could have forecast the judgment at hand. Well might this reflection concur with others to confirm the conclusion which the traditional accounts say the Roman centurion came to at the cross when he exclaimed, "Truly this was the son of God."

The memory of the character and mission of this historical Jesus would never die out; his mission took undebatable form in the minds of his disciples as a Messianic mission, while his personal qualities, both as a man and a seer, would, as they loomed larger through the increasing haze of tradition, be more and more referred to godhead and worshipped as divine. The Jewish nation had received no such warning from any preceding Jesus, and no prophet that preceded has shown such signs. Had the Pontius Pilate pretender been inflamed with such zeal, made display of such heroic virtue, and sounded forth such words, Judea was not the country where nor was that the time when the memory of them would all at once have died out. The Greeks and Romans of the day would have been quite as alert as the Jews, and would not have left such marvellous wonders to be first rehearsed by four obscure writers, who produced their accounts long after the events, and when all the contemporaries of the period were dead. Has not the world, we repeat, extant at this hour, all that contemporary men could know of the real character of him who was killed by Pontius Pilate, written too while the witnesses of the period were still alive?

But while we think we have given the soundest reasons to disprove the chronology which refers the death of Jesus to the procuratorship of Pilate, we are bound to confess that the character of the later historical Jesus is not ample enough to cover the conception given in the Gospels of the traditional Christ. Many reasonable persons will be ready to concede that this shortcoming augurs nothing against the theory we are broaching, seeing tradition is ever apt to add on incongruous elements, and those who report the tradition in this case stand convicted already of so many inconsistencies, falsehoods, and outrageous conceits, as to make the reception of their writings by the world an astonishment to all ingenuous men. For indeed is it not surprising that they should be received as true when they are self-contradictory, and accepted as so authoritative as to justify the denial of historic fact? What an anomaly that the Christian world should not only be deceived, but influenced by such palpably irrational writings! If the fact were not before our eyes, could we believe that men should pen, and others accept, the proposition that Jesus had no earthly father, while to prove his Messiahship a genealogical table is given to show that he was of the seed of David by being the son of Joseph, it being forgotten that a denial is therein involved of both the immaculate conception and the incarnation? If it is incredible that these two contradictions should be made, is it not far more incredible that they should be accepted, and that from age to age by thousands? Then, again, how can men persuade themselves that the Christ of these Gospels is true when the prophecy they made him utter respecting his return has failed so signally? And to how many other delusory and contradictory statements do the believers in these writings commit themselves? Verily if one were to enumerate all the vagaries and absurdities for which they are responsible, the world itself could not contain the books that should be written!

In such circumstances as these, we might stop short with the statement of our theory, and content ourselves with an appeal to what is recorded of the historical Jesus as explanatory of much that is peculiar to the traditional one; nay, we might even be allowed to have made good our point, had we found ourselves unable to complete the account. We have other historical material to refer to, however, and that we shall now bring under the reader's attention.

At the commencement of this chapter we referred to a certain duality of character which the Evangelical writers ascribe to the traditional Jesus. If they mention but one person, they at least ascribe to him attributes which can co-exist only in two separate natures, and are inconceivable in the unity of one and the same personality. No one who applies to the subject due reflection will long hesitate to admit this fact. Thus at one time we find him enforcing meekness and mercy, while at another his words are instinct with the harshest severity. "Ye have heard that it hath been said" (Matt. v. 43), he insists on one occasion, quoting a text as from the Bible, which is not there, "Thou shalt love thy *neighbour* and hate thine *enemy*. But I say unto you, Love your enemies, bless them that curse you, do good to them that hate you, and pray for them that despitefully use you, and persecute you." At another time this is what he says (Matt. x. 14-15), "And whosoever shall not receive you, nor hear your words, when ye depart out of that house or city, shake off the dust of your feet. Verily, I say unto you, it shall be more tolerable for the land of Sodom and Gomorrah in the day of judgment than for that city." And again, while we read this in Matt. ix. 18-20, "And when Jesus saw great multitudes about him, he gave commandment to depart unto the other side. And a certain scribe came and said unto him, Master, I will follow thee whithersoever thou goest. And Jesus saith unto him, The foxes have holes, and the birds of the air have nests, but the Son of man hath not where to lay his head;" it is immediately added verse 21, that "another of his disciples said unto him, *Lord, suffer me first to go and bury my father. But Jesus said unto him, Follow me, and let the dead bury their dead.*" The one who would follow, he bids go, for he is poor; the one who would go, he bids follow, even at the sacrifice of his natural affection. Is not this proof of a contradictory temper, a sign which points to the hypothesis of two personalities? At one time he insists on the eternal immutability of the Mosaic creed, and actually argues therefrom in assertion of the unity of God and his incommunicable goodness; at another he speaks of his gospel as the publication of a new law, and himself, not, like Moses, a servant, but the very son of the Most High.

It is not, then, a consistently meek and merciful character that is here portrayed to us. At times, indeed, and often, the loving, merciful nature comes into relief and wins us by its tenderness, but at others he wears an air quite out of keeping with that of the helpless one who inspires us with sympathy for his deep sorrows and his tragic fate. He who is alleged at one time to be poor and defenceless, is at another invested with a power to work miracles and relieve others' wants; he can turn water into wine, and multiply a few loaves and fishes so as to feed a host. Of no *one* character could such contradictory sentiments and actions be predicated; in no *one* living character could they by possibility unite. The man who could pray earnestly for mercy in behalf of his enemies, would not have cautioned his followers to provide themselves with swords. He whose meekness and mercifulness would not allow him to speak evil of his enemies could never be represented as an evil-doer, and under that accusation be put to death. Indeed it is impossible to conceive how such heterogeneous qualities should unite in *one person;* and it will be our business to furnish historical evidence to prove that the character conceived as one in tradition, and described as one by the four Greek writers, has resulted from identifying two separate historical personages, contemporaries of one another, who, as related by Josephus, lived in Judea under the procuratorship of Albinus, the one described by us as the meek prophet, and the other, as we shall show in our next chapter, a great innovator, who was escorted by a number of poor Galilean fishermen, who was *betrayed*, who had coadjutors and friends in the persons of *John* and *Simon*, both of whom *were imprisoned* and *released*, and who had to give to Josephus, as governor, seventy of the Galileans as hostages in pledge of peace.

CHAPTER XIII.

Archæology a forlorn hope—Delusions not credible because venerable—Despotisms and expected emancipations—The Missing-link—An anomaly—The Mosaic Jesus—Josephus' account of him—Parallels—Two persons described as one.

THE study of archæology has been prosecuted with great vigour in recent times, and memorials have been diligently sought for to verify the traditions of history, secular as well as sacred. Many striking confirmations of the traditions referred to have been thereby brought to light, and great and many have been the hopes that have sprung up in connection with these explorations. While this diligent search for truth continues, there is no sign, however, of any return to the state of things revealed by this disentombment. The march of improvement cannot be stayed, and the host moves on with increased and ever-increasing momentum. Meanwhile the more modern productions of the four Greek writers can expect no auxiliary aid from archæology. Time must first destroy the fabric they have reared before it can begin the work of reconstruction. It must bury out of sight the fables of the dead past, ere it can rear a temple worthy of the spirit, and this process is the prerogative of ages and ages, and cannot be furthered by dragging from their graves the skeletons and questioning the mummies of long-departed eras.

It would be saying too much were we to characterise the generation in which the four Greek writers lived as a more deluded one than our own. The religion these writers introduced was received only by a section, and a very small section, of their contemporaries, while the great intelligent bulk of the populations among whom their teachings took root, all accustomed though they were to the idea of a man-god, and the consequent idolatries, rejected the philosophy as a palpable delusion. We see something in our own days of the working of these fanatical enthusiasms. In Salt Lake city there is a hundred thousand of a population infected with such a fanaticism, all of whom to this day mourn the fate of the great founder of Mormonism with a sad regret, which, unless Mother Shipton's prophecy of the early end of the world come true, may prolong itself to remote generations. The world is not yet rid of imposture; whole communities, otherwise sane enough, are not proof against fits of temporary delirium; and yet the age is sound at the core in its judgment, and not capable of being longer seriously hoodwinked by any, however specious, passing deception. This exemption from error, however, applies only to the judgment of the present or immediate past, by no means to the views that are entertained of the earlier history of the world and the writings that record it; for it accepts as true to this day delusions and fanaticisms, by which only the ignorant were misled at the time of their first invention. How does it happen, we may ask, that we are so jealous of imposition to-day, and are so unwilling to confess we have been duped in regard to past deceptions? Would the present age for a moment entertain those delusions which it continues to accept as God's truth if they were attempted to be palmed off on it now, with no better evidence than was supplied at the time of their first introduction? And would not posterity be grievously misled if they should come to adopt as truth the delusions which the general sense of the present age rejects as convicted impostures? Yet this is precisely what has been done by the acceptance at the hands of the present generation of what at the introduction of Christianity was rejected by the great bulk of the intelligent world, and found favour with only a few of the ignorant multitude.

However, the present age is not so culpable as it seems, for indeed the past presses heavily on it by fortifying the delusions referred to with pains and penalties, and imposing them as authoritative alike on monarch and people; and there is the terrible anathema which pursues the man who dares to deny or distrust them. Happily the bonds are now relaxing, and it is to the distinguished honour of the English nation that they, by their disabilities legislation, have so bravely led the van in the work of emancipation. It is true, indeed, they are as zealous as ever in maintaining the philosophy that has been foisted on them by a deception they would now unanimously scorn, but they are content to support it now by mild exhortation, and by fostering at bottom the love of virtue and morality, which alone they hold ultimately venerable. Their conviction of the Christian faith is no doubt as genuine as ever, but this is because they cannot free themselves from the iron rule of tradition, and the despotism of a dogmatism the tyranny of which cannot be all at once and summarily discarded. What attitude such a nation will by and by assume, can be easily predicted. It will retain that affection for a high moral standard for which it has ever been distinguished. It will tolerate, nay, encourage, the search for honest truth, and, when that is discovered, it will manfully and indignantly spurn the fallacies of Christian fanaticism and superstition. In the hands of such a people the destiny of Christianity may be safely left; they will stand in the end by what of it is of God, and valorously cast overboard all in it that does not consist with reason and true loyalty.

That there is a missing link in the history of the Christian traditions, as given in the account of the four Greek writers, has, since the development of a very recent spirit of inquiry, been generally acknowledged. There is a greater desire evinced to find this missing link, ever since historical inquiry has demonstrated the fact that the Gospels were not written

L

till the second century. The difficulty to which we refer as still unresolved is this: How such events as those recorded in the Gospels could have happened and escape the observation of the public at the time, and all notice at the hands of the historians of the period? That the Almighty God should have visited the earth, performing godlike actions, both on earth and in the heavens, beyond the power of man to effect, in the sight of a nation—a nation, too, in a peculiar frame of mind, on the tiptoe of expectation for the advent of their Messiah—*without its being aware of any of these wonderful occurrences*, presents an anomaly which we think has not only not been explained, but has not received the attention it calls for. The fact cannot be too often affirmed and re-affirmed, so long as mankind are still held by the spell of a huge delusion, that the more numerous the miracles are which are referred to the period of Pontius Pilate's procuratorship, the weaker is the historical ground in support of them. Public wonders cannot be concealed, or, if they could, would not be public. Now, it is of this period the most wonderful events are related that have happened in the world since the Mosaic age, and the account of them was first published in the second century after their alleged occurrence, when no living witnesses were alive to deny or affirm their reality. Fortunately there is a contemporary history of the time extant to which we can appeal, and which substantively denies these traditional averments, which must either have lain concealed from the eye of the world till then, or been first concocted at the time of their publication? If they existed before, how could they be kept in concealment? Is it usual with historians to keep back the most wonderful, the most public, and the most important historical transactions, and to make the most of the least significant and important?

Our argument, however, does not hinge entirely on the want of historical evidence for these events, weighty as the force may be of this negative demonstration. That indeed is unanswerable in its way; but we profess also to refute the accounts in debate by *direct* as well as indirect probation, and by the inexorable logic of facts to maintain that whatever grounds there may be and are for the assertions the accounts in question make in regard to the events of a later period, these events did *not* occur in the age of Pontius Pilate.

It is now time we should refer to that other Jesus of whom Josephus writes as contemporary with himself and the "meek" one, of whose character and fate he gives so touching a description. In calling attention to this second Jesus we would request our readers to remark how it is the manner of the four Greek writers to blend different characters together and describe them as one; and not characters only, but incidents; in such combination, too, that it is next to impossible to sunder the confusion and disentangle the actual facts. The characters and actions they describe are not such as could possibly centre in one personality; and this is especially the case with the central personage in their story; the explanation of which is, that they have confounded *two* notable contemporaries of the same name into *one*. Certain traditions spoke of the one, some of the other, till at length the two got blended, and the characters, actions, and incidents peculiar to each separately were predicated of one only. One of these was, as we have seen, a meek personage, who suffered torture for prophesying evil to the nation, and whose idiosyncrasies were of a peculiar, nay, extraordinary order. The other Jesus, whose life and fortunes are blended with his, was of a totally different character. By way of distinguishing the one from the other, we will describe the poor oppressed one, who proved himself to be a true prophet, as the *spiritual* Jesus, and the other as the *Mosaic* Jesus, because we consider him as the prototype of the severe side of the character of the traditional Jesus, as it appears in his zeal for the law of Moses. The description of this Mosaic Jesus is chiefly given in the autobiography of Josephus, although it is also slightly referred to in his History of the Wars. This Jesus, with his coadjutors John and Simon, are introduced to us in connection with an insurrection in Galilee against the Roman authority. Josephus himself was at that time governor of the province, and in his wisdom endeavouring, in the interest of Rome, to reconcile his fellow-countrymen to its rule. This policy of his was inconsistent with that of those who had other interests, and a confederacy was formed which sought unscrupulously to damage his government and procure his recall. This then was the situation when a collapse was brought about by the *betrayal* of Jesus and the incarceration of John and of Simon, the angel of whose release appears to have been none other than the magnanimous governor himself, from whose account of the matter we must now quote.*

" Now, as soon as I was come into Galilee, and had learned this state of things by the information of such as told me of them, I wrote to the Sanhedrim at Jerusalem about them, and required their direction what I should do. Their direction was, that I should continue there, and that if my fellow-legates were willing, I should join with them in the care of Galilee. But those my fellow-legates, having gotten great riches from those tithes which as priests were their dues, and were given to them, determined to return to their own country. Yet when I desired them to stay so long, that we might first settle the public affairs, they complied with me. So I removed, together with them, from the city of Sepphoris, and came to a certain village called Bethmaus, four furlongs distant from Tiberias; and thence I sent messengers to the senate of Tiberias, and desired that the principal men of the city would come to me; and when they were come, Justus himself being also with them, I told them that I was sent to them by the people of Jerusalem as a legate, together with these other priests, in order to persuade them to demolish that house which Herod the Tetrarch had built there, and which had the figures of living creatures in it, although our laws have forbidden us to make any such figures; and I

* Life of Josephus, Secs. 12–14.

desired that they would give us leave so to do immediately. But for a good while Capellus and the principal men belonging to the city would not give us leave, but were at length entirely overcome by us, and were induced to be of our opinion. So *Jesus* the son of Sapphias, *one of those, whom we have already mentioned as the leader of a seditious tumult of mariners and poor people*, prevented us, and took with him certain *Galileans*, and set the entire palace on fire, and thought he should get a great deal of money thereby, because he saw some of the roofs gilt with gold. They also plundered a great deal of the furniture, which was done without our approbation; for, after we had discoursed with Capellus and the principal men of the city, we departed from Bethmaus, and went into Upper Galilee. But Jesus and his party slew all the Greeks that were inhabitants of Tiberias, and as many others as were their enemies before the war began.

"When I understood this state of things, I was greatly provoked, and went down to Tiberias, and took all the care I could of the royal furniture, to recover all that could be recovered from such as had plundered it. They consisted of candlesticks made of Corinthian brass, and of royal tables, and of a great quantity of uncoined silver; and I resolved to preserve whatsoever came to my hand for the king. So I sent for ten of the principal men of the senate, and for Capellus, the son of Antyllus, and committed the furniture to them, with this charge, that they should part with it to nobody else but to myself. From thence I and my fellow-legates went to Gischala, to John, as desirous to know his intentions, and soon saw that he was for innovations, and had a mind to the principality, for he desired me to give him authority to carry off that corn which belonged to Cæsar and lay in the villages of Upper Galilee; and

he pretended that he would expend what it came to
in building the walls of his own city. But when I
perceived what he endeavoured at, and what he had
in his mind, I said I would not permit him so to do,
for that I thought either to keep it for the Romans
or myself, now that I was intrusted with public
affairs there by the people of Jerusalem. But, when he
was not able to prevail with me, he betook himself
to my fellow-legates; for they had no sagacity in
providing for futurity, and were very ready to take
bribes. So he corrupted them with money to decree,
that all that corn which was within his province
should be delivered to him; while I, who was but
one, was outvoted by two, and held my tongue.
Then did John introduce another cunning contrivance
of his; for he said that those Jews who inhabited
Cæsarea Philippi, and were shut up by the order of
the king's deputy there, had sent to him to desire
him, that, since they had no oil that was pure for
their use, he would provide a sufficient quantity of
such oil that came from the Greeks, and thereby
transgress their own laws. Now this was said by
John, not out of his regard to religion, but out of his
most flagrant desire of gain, for he knew that two
sextaries were sold with them of Cæsarea for one
drachma; but that at Gischala fourscore sextaries were
sold for four sextaries. So he gave order that all the
oil which was there should be carried away, as having
my permission for so doing; which yet I did not
grant him voluntarily, but only out of fear of the
multitude; since, if I had forbidden him, I should
have been stoned by them. When I had therefore
permitted this to be done by John, he gained vast
sums of money by this his knavery. But when I had
dismissed my fellow-legates, and sent them back to
Jerusalem, I took care to have arms provided, and
the cities fortified. And when I had sent for the

most hardy among the robbers, I saw that it was not in my power to take their arms from them ; but I persuaded the multitude to allow them money as pay, and told them it was better for them to give them a little willingly, rather than (be forced to) to overlook them, while they plundered their goods from them. And when I had obliged them to take an oath not to come into that country, unless they were invited to come, or else when they had not their pay given them, I dismissed them, and charged them neither to make an expedition against the Romans, nor against those their neighbours that lay round about them ; for my first care was to keep Galilee in peace. So I was willing to have the principal of the *Galileans, in all seventy*, as hostages for their fidelity, but still under the notion of friendship. Accordingly I made them my friends and companions as I journeyed, and *set them to judge causes ;* and with their approbation it was that I gave my sentences, while I endeavoured not to mistake what justice required, and to keep my hands clear of all bribery in those determinations."

While we admit it is desirable and necessary that our readers should consult the pages of history for themselves in order to discover and estimate the exact amount of historical truth at the basis of the traditional narratives, it is still necessary for us, in order to impart connection to our argument, that we should relate the attitude assumed and the action taken by John, Simon, and Jesus in this case against Josephus, while at the same time we transfer to our pages such historical verifications as may tend to the identification of these historical characters with those which have come down to us in the traditions of later ages. Thus far we have in the above quotations, it appears, a substantial parallel between the character of this Jesus and the incidents of his life and certain marked features given in the traditional narratives. Jesus is the leader of *poor people* and *mariners* (*alias* fishermen); the people are *Galileans*, *seventy* of whom are accepted as semi-hostages for their good behaviour, who, nevertheless, are permitted to *journey about* and give decisions in questions of *religion*, for the laws of the land were the laws of God, the laying down of which might be described as teaching. These facts are similar to those mentioned in the Gospels, and are no doubt identical with them. We will not lay much stress upon John's trickery to obtain the *corn* and the *oil*, and the coincidence between the mention of them here and the reference to those articles afterwards in certain parallel circumstances in the book of Revelation.

In order to make clearer the conspiracy of John, Jesus, and Simon against the authority of Josephus, we must quote a passage or two more from his autobiography (secs. 21, 22):—

"But now another great number of the Galileans came together again, with their weapons, as knowing the man (John) how wicked and how sadly perjured he was, and desired me to lead them against him, and promised me that they would actually destroy both him and Gischala. Hereupon I professed that I was obliged to them for their readiness to serve me, and that I would more than requite their good-will to me. However I entreated them to restrain themselves, and begged of them to give me leave to do what I intended, which was to put an end to these troubles without bloodshed; and when I had prevailed with the multitude of the Galileans to let me do so, I came to Sepphoris. But the inhabitants of this city, having determined to continue in their allegiance to the Romans, were afraid of my coming to them, and tried by putting me upon another action to divert me, that they might be freed from the terror they were in. Accordingly they sent to *Jesus*, the captain of those robbers who were in the confines of Ptolemaïs, and promised to give him a great deal of money, if he would come with those forces he had with him, which were in number eight hundred, and fight with us. Accordingly he complied with what they desired, upon the promises they had made him, and was desirous to fall upon us, when we were unprepared for him, and knew nothing of his coming beforehand. So he sent to me, and desired that I would give him leave to come and salute me. When I had given him that leave, which I did without the least knowledge of his treacherous intentions beforehand, he took his band of robbers, and made haste to come to me. Yet did not this knavery succeed well at last; for as he was already nearly approaching, *one of those with him deserted him, and came to me and told me what he had undertaken to do.* When I was informed of this, I went into the market-place, and pretended to know nothing of his treacherous purpose. I took with me many Galileans that were armed, as also some of those of Tiberias; and when I had given orders that all the roads should be carefully guarded, I charged the keepers of the gates to give admittance to none but Jesus when he came, with the principal of his men, and to exclude the rest, and in case they aimed to force themselves in, to use stripes (in order to repel them). Accordingly those that had received such a charge did as they were bidden, and *Jesus came in with a few others*, and when I had ordered him to throw down his arms immediately, and told him that if he refused so to do he was a dead man, he, seeing armed men standing all about him, was terrified and complied; and as for those of his followers that were excluded, when they were informed that he was *seized, they ran away*. I then called Jesus to me by himself, and told him that I was not a stranger to that treacherous design he had against me, nor was I ignorant by whom he was sent for; that, however, I would forgive him what he had done already if he would repent of it, and be faithful to me hereafter. And thus, upon his promise to do all that I desired, I let him go, and gave him leave to get those whom he had formerly had with him together again. But I threatened the inhabitants of Sepphoris, that, if they would not leave off their ungrateful treatment of me, I would punish them sufficiently."

Here we have historical mention of that Jesus who was the friend of Simon and John, and had as his followers "*poor Galileans, mariners*, who were in his pay," one of whom *had betrayed him to Josephus*, the priest and governor, and all of whom fled when they knew he was seized. These no doubt are the same facts which were by and by incorporated in the traditional accounts, and connected with the history of Jesus of Nazareth.

And let no one spurn the derivation we allege, as though in making it we laid ourselves open to the charge of irreverence; the accusation can be brought with equal reason against the Evangelists themselves, one of them deemed the most accurate, and the other reputed the best beloved of his master.

In St. Luke xxii. 34-36 we read :—

"And he said, I tell thee, Peter, the cock shall not crow this day, before that thou shalt thrice deny that thou knowest me. And he said unto them, *When I sent you without purse, and scrip, and shoes, lacked ye anything?* And they said, Nothing. *Then said he unto them, But now, he that hath a purse, let him take it and likewise his scrip; and he that hath no sword, let him sell his garment and buy one.*"

This is the address of Jesus to his followers *just before the arrival of the multitude* sent to arrest him at the instance of the chief priest, into whose hands he was betrayed; and it is evidently suggested by the memory of the circumstances in which his prototype found himself when about to be betrayed into the hands of the governor of Galilee. Both the historical and the traditional narratives record two identical facts: that Jesus was betrayed by one of his followers, and that he was abandoned and shamefully deserted by the rest of them. It might have been reasonably concluded that in such a situation he came by his end, though he was in fact permitted by Josephus to return to his followers.

But into this point we need not enter too critically. There is a general reflection in this relation of more importance for us than such small details, which cannot affect the main question. The great point of our inquiry at present is the moral character of Jesus;

and whether we look to the historical spiritual Jesus, whom we have described as pre-eminently meek, who suffered at the hands of man the direst torture, without one word of denunciation except the denunciation of impending destruction, or whether we look to the meek side of the Jesus whose loving mercy is depicted in the pages of the Greek Evangelists, what we maintain is that it is impossible to accept the characteristics quoted above as the characteristics of either of these, and that therefore the narrative of the four Greek writers describes two persons. No one person, if sane, could by any possibility exhibit such contradictory features. Look, for instance, at the language he uses on the eve of his betrayal. The followers of Jesus were insufficiently armed, and being believed by him to have, some of them money, some a scrip, some a garment to dispose of, they were urged by him, if reduced to the last extremity, to sell their garment and buy a sword. This could not be for ornament; for that purpose garments are generally more serviceable; it could only be that a sword would, in the circumstances then imminent, be of greater use. How ingeniously he is made to refer to the period when first his followers entered his service! Though they had, he reminded them, neither "purse," nor "scrip," nor even "shoes," yet they had lacked nothing. If, then, they had none of these things when they entered his service, it would not be so great a sacrifice if they should part at his bidding, and in his interest, with these now to supply the present need.

A more ingenious speech could not be conceived to induce a body of men to act in the way desired; for the exhortation reminds them of the speaker's power to provide for them in the future since he had done so in the past, and that they were only asked to dispose of those things they had received in his service.

Now it is plain that this procedure on the part of the traditional Jesus is altogether inconsistent and quite irreconcilable with the character ascribed to the meek, long-suffering Jesus of Josephus. Indeed, it is impossible that he who is described in the Gospels as a tender-hearted, loving teacher, whose whole life was spent in pitying misery and relieving distress, and who could at lowest be looked upon by others as a mystic and enthusiast, should ever be charged as a malefactor and arraigned as a criminal, had it not been for the tradition concerning his namesake who believed in the sword, and the call of a man to wield it in the cause of the Almighty.

Here is the charge which was brought against him (John xviii. 29, 30):—"Pilate then went out unto them, and said, What accusation bring ye against this man? They answered and said unto him, *If he were not a malefactor*, we would not have delivered him up unto thee." Is it conceivable that such a charge as this should be made against the meek Jesus, whose only offence was warning his countrymen of coming evil, and who is uniformly represented in the evangelical tradition as giving life and not destroying it? On the other hand, this is the very charge which history records was brought against his contemporary, the friend of John and Simon, and who was just such a man as to earn the title "malefactor" here given him by John, being he who, according to Luke, urged his followers to sell their garments and procure swords. These deeds are not historically charged against the meek Jesus, who was more sinned against than sinning; they were the actions of another Jesus, who was in reality an evil-doer. It is the four Greek writers who charge the meek, merciful Jesus with these crimes, and not the historian of the period.

Josephus tells us that there were two men of the same name, both notable and living at the same time, and that a time when portents and prodigies of a striking kind amazed the Judean world; that the one was inspired with the belief that he was a prophet, and was, in fact, instinct with a certain "divine fury;" that he preached a gospel of woe through the length and breadth of the land; and though they tried and again tried to torture him into silence, they could not persuade him to desist. The other Jesus, Josephus tells us, though of kindred pretensions, was a man of a stern, uncompromising spirit, and sought other ends, who was forsaken by all his followers after having been betrayed by one of them. Now it is the characters of these two men as described by Josephus which we think gave rise to the conception of the traditional Jesus, while the capital mistake committed by the Evangelists in their chronology is, we think, due to a further confusion in the Greek mind of this

Jesus with the prophet who suffered under Pontius Pilate.

Thus the traditional narratives are at fault in antedating the time of the events and in combining two historical characters into one being, while the theological instinct has at the same time resolved the one back into two by representing the being in question as partaker at once of the divine and the human natures. Thus there are two theoretical barriers to the reception of this Christ; the one moral, due to incompatibility of character, and the other physical, due to incompatibility of nature.

At this point it is for the reader to say whether the man described by Luke as a man of the sword, and arraigned in John as a malefactor, so unlike in these and others respects to the meek martyr of Jerusalem, is, as the Gospels allege, God Almighty Himself, or only a fanatical echo of the physical-force reformer of Galilee. Is not this last the original side of the character of him who is described as having fishermen for followers, and as betrayed into the hands of the rulers, and his woe-struck contemporary the original of the other side of the same being, who is represented as meek and lowly of heart? For is there not in this one image two natures, so utterly opposed to each other as to be absolutely irreconcilable? And can any one read the narratives of the four Greek writers without having his sense of the excellency of the character dashed at every turn by the ascription of contradictory attributes or actions? No one who studies attentively these records can fail to note this inconsistency, however much he may be persuaded that the authors believed they were relating the life and fortunes of one character. Anyhow, all this inquiry proves that most of the traditional statements have a basis in prior historical relations, and this fact is an evidence of the desire of the writers to compose a narrative of actual occurrences. And, with all their proneness to endow him they worship with miraculous gifts, it is noticeable that while they make him turn water into wine, and multiply a few loaves so that they feed thousands, they stop short of ascribing to him the power to create or multiply swords, and of representing him as himself supplying the need of his disciples with heaven-tempered ones out of his own armoury.

Josephus supplies further details of the character of this Galilean Jesus, who, we see throughout, is quite innocent of the meekness ascribed to his notable compeer. We cannot, of course, transcribe these details here, and must content ourselves with referring the reader to Josephus himself. One extract more, however, we shall give from his pages bearing on this notable character.

Josephus says in sec. 27 of his autobiography:*—

"Now when all Galilee was filled with this rumour, that their country was about to be betrayed by me to the Romans, and when all men were exasperated against me, and ready to bring me to punishment,

* Life of Josephus.

the inhabitants of Tarichæe did also themselves suppose that what the young men said was true, and persuaded my guards and armed men to leave me when I was asleep, and to come presently to the hippodrome, in order there to take counsel against me their commander. And when they had prevailed with them, and they were gotten together, they found there a great company assembled already, who all joined in one clamour, to bring the man who was so wicked to them as to betray them, to his due punishment; and it was *Jesus, the son of Sapphius, who principally set them on. He was ruler in Tiberias, a wicked man, and naturally disposed to make disturbances in matters of consequence; a seditious person he was indeed, and an innovator beyond everybody else. He then took the laws of Moses into his hands, and came into the midst of the people, and said, 'O my fellow-citizens, if you are not disposed to hate Josephus on your own account, have regard however to these laws of your country, which your commander-in-chief is going to betray; hate him therefore on both these accounts, and bring the man who hath acted thus insolently to his deserved punishment.'*"

This language consists with what the traditional Jesus says, so much *in opposition to his other utterances*, as to the imperishability of the law of Moses, and is quite in keeping with the harsh demand he made on one to follow him who pled to be allowed to go first and bury his father. So that we see, however much inconsistencies abound in the traditional reports, there is reason to believe that, if we except the philosophy they were adduced to support, none of the features of these accounts were the work of invention, but had all their basis in some fact or other, recorded or unrecorded, in the history of the period. There was no intention to deceive, only at worst a weak credulity at work in hearts prostrate before the allegation of a preternatural epiphany, itself the product of a wild enthusiasm that sprung up like an *ignis fatuus* on the eve of a great dissolution.

CHAPTER XIV.

How the name of Jesus supplanted that of Judas—Josephus silent about the Pontius Pilate Jesus—Gives the true genesis of the story—His account of his historical labours—The Evangelists stultify themselves—History to be respected, solecisms to be rejected.

IN our last chapter we introduced our readers to the account which Josephus gives of the Galilean Jesus and his followers, and how, when our historian was in authority in the district, that impostor stirred up the people against him, and charged him, in his policy of submission to Rome, with betraying the law of Moses and subverting the theocratic government which he had sanctified the Jew to set up. The machinations of this man and his coadjutors caused Josephus no small trouble, and it was only by his own wit and energy he was able so to use the power he was invested with as to escape out of their hands. By these means his enemies were outwitted and captured, and then released in a way to satisfy them of his own power and their impotence to resist. And all this is related by him in a manner such as to establish an identity between his narrative and a chapter in the traditional accounts.

At this time Josephus was a man of thirty, and

the authority he held was a priestly one, subject to the Roman Government. To throw off the yoke of this last, the people had been stirred up, mainly by the philosophy of the sect founded by Judas of Galilee, and they were now led on by this Galilean Jesus, who proved himself to be the greatest of all innovators, a seditious person, appealing to the laws of Moses in justification of his action and advice. This new philosophy of Judas of Galilee, which was in reality opposed to true Mosaic principles, had exercised a great influence over the *younger sort*, who took it up enthusiastically, and, among the rest, this Jesus, who preached it forth prophetically, got multitudes to follow him, and essayed to propagate it by the sword, with such zeal that *his name*, and not Judas's, who was now dead, was handed down to posterity as that of the founder of the new faith. That Judas was the founder we know on the unimpeachable authority of Josephus, but it was perfectly natural his name should in the traditional reports be merged and lost in that of his zealous disciple, so that it is as easy to account for the change of name as for the chief error in the chronology, and the blending into one of this fiery enthusiast for the law and the meek martyr of Jerusalem.

The genesis of these errors may be easily traced by reference to the pages of Josephus, who has been proved to be the most reliable historian by men of the greatest learning and the soundest judgment, from the first publication of his work down to the present time. Josephus needs no tribute from our pen; his reputation for truth and accuracy is universally acknowledged, and the force of an appeal to his testimony is such as to defy all contradiction. When he was governor of Galilee he must have met with many who were alive during the procuratorship of Pilate, whose recall took place just thirty years before; that is, therefore, at the time he himself was born. All those who were upwards of thirty years of age must have been witnesses of the wonderful events which are recorded in the Gospels as having in their day taken captive the Galilean world; and he must have heard of these events from them or their children, if they ever happened. If so, some of them must have shared in the multiplication of the loaves or witnessed the miraculous draught of fishes; as their contemporaries of Judea might have been able to testify of the raising of Lazarus. Many of them might have known, too, of the lame who had been made to walk and the blind who had been made to see. Nay, it is reasonable to presume there were multitudes who were acquainted with the relations of Jesus. Or are we to believe that all these things were familiarly known by sense or hearsay to every native of the district, but kept hid from the intelligent governor, who was wide-awake all the while, taking notes too to "print" them? Josephus fills his pages with the story of this fanatical Jesus and his imbecile crew, whom he treats so lightly as to set them at large again after their arrest, as of no political account, yet knows nothing and says nothing, forsooth, of that other, whom multitudes wandered after while he lived, and who was now worshipped as a god since his death, by zealous, far-spreading communities! He carefully, conscientiously, and patiently traces the history of the nation from its roots, ransacks all records and examines all witnesses to get at the facts, reports with minuter and minuter detail the events of his own day and of that of his father, is at pains to describe the religion of Judas of Galilee, with the fanaticism he inspired and the turmoil and trouble his followers caused in society, and condescends to notice the most insignificant personages and events, whose connection with the movement afoot was often only of the remotest character, supplying in regard to some of these particulars enough, if it were worth, to complete a rounded biography; he tells us, as we have seen, of the impostor of Samaria, who came to grief, both himself and his followers, and brought the procurator into disgrace with his superiors; he tells of the meek martyr who brought woe upon himself in denouncing woe upon the people; and he tells, finally, of him whose cause so collapsed that he and his band were glad to accept forgiveness at his own hands as governor;—and all this, not as the Evangelists, who blunder at every turn, but with the graphic power of an immediate witness; and all the while he says nothing of the Jesus who wrought such wonders and died on a cross under Pilate, to whose earthly life, notwithstanding, Christendom looks back with believing regard as the incarnation of deity.

Yet to him, who both lived in and wrote of the time, and not to those who lived and wrote generations after, must we look for the facts of the period; and if the events related by the Evangelists have any historical basis at all, that must be sought for in his pages,—a proceeding which the study of the Evangelists themselves justifies; for however much they differ from him as to time, their accounts and his agree in the leading incidents, as witness this single coincidence, how both they and he make Jesus foretell his own death, go up to Jerusalem to meet it, and offer himself there in sacrifice for the sins of the people.

Now let us hear what account Josephus himself gives of his historical labours. He says (Book xx. c. 11, § 2) :—

"I shall now, therefore, make an end here of my Antiquities; after the conclusion of which events, I began to write that account of the war; and these Antiquities contain what hath been delivered down to us from the original creation of man *until the twelfth year of the reign of Nero*, as to what hath befallen the Jews, as well in Egypt as in Syria *and in Palestine*, and what we have suffered from the Assyrians and Babylonians, and what afflictions the Persians and Macedonians, and after them the Romans, have brought upon us; *for I think I may say that I have composed this history with sufficient accuracy in all things.* I have attempted to enumerate those high-priests that we have had during the interval of two thousand years. I have also carried down the succession of our kings, and related their actions and political administration without errors, as also the power of our monarchs; and all according to what is written in our sacred books; for this it was that I promised to do in the beginning of this history, *and I am so bold as to say, now I have so completely perfected the work I proposed to myself to do, that no other person, whether he were a Jew or a foreigner, had he ever so great an inclination to it, could so accurately deliver these accounts to the Greeks as is done in these books.* For those of my own nation freely acknowledge that I far exceed them in the learning belonging to the Jews. I have also taken a great deal of pains to attain the learning of the Greeks, and understand the elements of the Greek language, although I have so long accustomed myself to speak our own tongue that I cannot pronounce Greek with sufficient exactness, for our nation does not encourage those that learn the languages of many nations, and so adorn their discourses with the smoothness of their periods, because they look upon this sort of accomplishment as common, not only to all sorts of freemen, but to as many of the servants as please to learn them. But they give him the testimony of being a wise man who is fully acquainted with our laws and is able to interpret their meaning; on which account, as there have been many who have done their endeavours with great patience to obtain this learning, there have yet hardly been so many as two or three that have succeeded therein, who were immediately well rewarded for their pains."

In these books, while he makes mention of prophets true and false, he denies, writing fifty years after the recall of Pilate, that any new sect had arisen among the Jews except the sect of Judas of Galilee, and it is impossible to account for the reputation he had for historical fidelity if it be true that there existed another founded by Jesus of Nazareth. Nor is it any fault of his that the traditional accounts ignore Judas and speak only of Jesus. About this Jesus he is, as we have seen, explicit enough, and no one who had studied his account could have fallen into the post-historical blunder. Neither, had they taken their cue from him, could the Evangelists have confounded the victim of the Pontius Pilate policy with the Jesus of history. He was a Samaritan and not a Galilean; he lived in a period marked by no portent, prodigy, or miraculous sign; and not one fact is recorded of him, as of the other two, to identify him with the Jesus of tradition, except the fact of his having suffered under Pilate. Moreover, had the Evangelists consulted Josephus, they would have found that the Jesus whom they supposed to be one was really two, and they might have concluded from him, had they thought, that only in the light of this fact could the inconsistencies in the character be reconciled to reason.

As we read the traditional accounts, the conviction is forced upon us that the writers in their simplicity believed they were recording what had escaped the notice of the historians of the day, and that but for them the facts they relate would never have been reported in the ear of the world; as if this fact did not directly undermine the ground on which they stood and contradict their explicit assertions. But it is not true, as they assume, that they only are the witnesses of the facts related, for not only, as we have seen, does the historian of the day record events of vastly inferior importance, but he actually gives the lie direct to the assertions they make, that the transactions they relate happened under the procuratorship of Pilate, and that the founder of the new faith was Jesus of Nazareth, who, according to Luke's testimony, must have been only a stripling in years at the period of Pilate's recall from the governorship. And who shall say what other contradictions to their historical witness-bearing his pages may yield when once these are studied in relation to the question in hand, and with the respect due to a man who had such opportunity of knowing the facts of the period, and no interest to serve by concealment or extenuation?

Meanwhile, let us ask ourselves if it was fair and likely to serve the cause of truth that their writings should have been at the first respected and his neglected, and whether it is right that we should continue to prefer their far-off report to his direct, almost ocular evidence? It was wrong for the compilers of the traditional accounts to construct their story on the vague hearsay of traditional report, when there already lay to hand, in the very tongue in which they wrote, a record by one who could not but know familiarly all the particulars; and it is our bounden duty to do what we can to repair the wrong, and set ourselves right with the facts of history. What would we think of an author who, on the hearsay evidence of the third or fourth generation, should vamp up a life of the first Napoleon, in which all the facts were thrown topsyturvy, and the dates flung back a quarter of a century, and profess that his was the only reliable account, in ignorance of all that had been already written and published to the contrary; and what if he should make the first Napoleon promise that he would return again, and yet, though he wrote after the event, take no note of the fulfilment of the promise in the appearance of the second? Or what, again, would we think of the historian supposed, if he confounded the first with the second, and transferred the events in the life of the latter to the career of the former? For this is what the Greek writers have done in regard to events of much more account than any that have taken place in the history of the world: they have referred events and incidents which occurred towards the fall of Jerusalem to the days of Pilate, and though they make the Pontius Pilate prophet utter predictions in regard to his return, they not only take no note of the events amidst which his return was expected, but they write in utter unconsciousness of all that transpired; they do *not know* that the story they write respects two men of totally opposite character, who first made their appearance in this latter period.

And can any character be more self-contradictory than that of him whom they describe as teaching at once brotherly love and brotherly hatred, requiring filial respect and filial disrespect, such as is involved in leaving a father unburied, spurning the homage of his mother and kindred and opening his arms to strangers, proclaiming himself a king and declining the honours of royalty, armed with power to relieve the wants of others and himself without a place where to lay his own head, sacrificing his life to save some and jealous lest others should taste of his salvation, equalling himself to God and disclaiming a title to goodness, praying for those that scourged him and bidding his followers provide themselves with swords, opening heaven to a malefactor suffering his doom, and representing it as impossible for a rich man to get there as for a camel to go through the eye of a needle, and receiving sinners and eating with them while he consigns honourable and respectable men to eternal perdition? Can a character with inconsistencies so gross be palmed off on reasonable men as an incarnation of Deity? Is it not high time all men should unite and shake off the incubus of a superstition so baleful?

CHAPTER XV.

A distorting medium—Our feelings exaggerative—Josephus' record not to be set aside—Herod's grandfather and grandson confounded—The Gospels not mythical—Plagiarisms—The whole a "mélange."

It lay in the nature of the case that the four Greek writers, who record traditional statements without regard to chronological order, should blend the characters and events they describe exactly as we have in preceding chapters shown they did. They blended the characters of the two Jesuses, and described them as *one*, all unconscious of the antagonistic impossible elements they had made to meet in one personality. Yet the embodiment, as portrayed, discloses a contradiction that would have rendered such a character odious, if the claim of divinity on the one hand and fanatic zeal on the other had not hidden the discordance. Only an analysis of the character could break the spell and reveal the extremes, that could not unite and form one homogeneous nature.

The account of the meek Jesus given by Josephus may be called dramatic history, but when embellished in tradition by combination with the character and the events in the life of the other, it becomes dramatic history combined with fiction. The former is infinitely preferable, although much less sensational. The vices when thus combined with the virtues escape recognition, and even superstitions, fanaticisms, and contradictions become invested with a certain halo of sacredness. It is so the Christian has come to regard the picture given in the Gospels; hence he shrinks from *examining it too closely*, and, in fact, from analysing it at all, and he falls before the character portrayed as a paragon of perfection to be only worshipped. The whole is viewed erelong as a heavenly and an earthly combination, the perfections being referred to the former, and the imperfections to the latter, until at length it presents a figure before which every other sinks into insignificance, and historical reality is lost in the indiscriminate glamour. And when cooler judgments remonstrated that the promise held out in the story had failed for want of fulfilment, the cunning subterfuge was resorted to of referring its accomplishment to a later time or another sphere of existence; and it was boldly maintained that the throne of David, which was to be set up on earth in time, had been transferred to the skies to be revealed in eternity; all because four Greeks had been cozened into the belief, and had persuaded the rest of the world, that an inconsistent character was God, and would not disappoint those who trusted in him. And yet the whole story is a mad farrago, conglomerated together by confounding period with period, incident with incident, person with person, man with God, and God in him with God in reality.

We have endeavoured to some extent to disconnect the traditional links which bound together into one the two Jesuses, and we have shown that the imagined traditional unity is a compound of two personalities. They are to be seen as *two separate* individuals in *history*, and turn up as one individual first in *tradition*. The moral character of the one nature, that of the meek sufferer, is tarnished by the blending of the defects of the other, that of the violent innovator, and the disharmony first appears when we have resolved the two into distinct persons. Till this is done, however, the heavenly attributes ascribed to the one blind the eye to the earthly qualities of the other and the fact of a blending. The display of meek, loving qualities in the martyr, whose sorrows are great, attracts our generous sympathies, and we have not the heart to condemn those other qualities which appear in combination, however heterogeneous, all the more when the character is presented to us as a divine manifestation; yet it is never to be forgotten that truth is ever in great danger of falling a sacrifice to excess of sympathy. What if the dramatic interest be lessened by the application of a remorseless logic to the fact? Should we not therefore feel comforted that we have thereby got rid of a delusion, which is a snare, and that in this case we have been taught to cast away an impossible idol and set up again in our hearts the proper worship of the living God? The meek Jesus is not responsible for all this abuse and idolatry. He suffered because his countrymen resented his warning of woe and the implied condemnation; and if his prophetic utterances are to be judged by their fulfilment, he must be acknowledged to have been a prophet. The "divine fury" or passion ascribed to him by the historian testifies impressively to the effect of his mission upon his contemporaries. Indeed the pages of Josephus yield the only historical account the world to this hour possesses of the impression made by that "divine fury" of his on the minds of his contemporaries, and his appearance at the time in the Judean world. This historian is the first to announce this character and the events of his wonderful career, and his is exactly the character and life which we find referred in the Evangelical accounts to the Pontius Pilate period.

It is difficult to explain how all this travestie of history arose, whether from a design to mislead, or simply in the interest of a peculiar philosophy; but once accepted as the groundwork of a world-religion, its historical truth was maintained as a matter of necessity, and it was erelong regarded as the fruit of divine inspiration. Anyhow, the Jesus of the period, which coincides with the fall of the Jewish state, is the only Jesus of history described as a prophet possessed by a *divine fury*, as having suffered for his fidelity in warning his countrymen of their fate, as having foretold the destruction of the Temple, the city, and the people, as having undergone public trials before the Sanhedrim and the tribunal of the Roman procurator, as having been fed by the people, as, owing to his weird enthusiasm and preternatural gravity, having been looked upon as insane, and as dying like a martyr out of zeal for his country; and these are the very characteristics which, along with those of his contemporary, distinguish the Jesus of the traditional narratives.

These four Greek writers or their original authorities seem to have had a great talent for combination; and what we have already said of them in that respect is not imaginary, but capable of proof as true, which our readers, we presume, will expect us to show them. To these four writers and to Paul the world is indebted for the most wonderful imaginary combination of events that has ever yet been foisted on it for acceptance in the name of history. Nothing, however, of all they tell was published at the time of its occurrence, and the historians of the day, although they relate other events of insignificant importance, are absolutely silent respecting one and all of these as having happened within the period alleged; they only mention the principal of them as having taken place years after, and thus unconsciously confirm the anachronous and manufactured traditional narratives. The only prophet of whom there is any record as belonging to the Pontius Pilate period is a totally different character from the subject of this Evangelical story, and his existence is testified to by

Josephus, when his statement, if false, could have been contradicted by thousands, but was not.

Perhaps some sublime theologians, having succeeded in abolishing *the laws of Moses*, on the ground that they were of force only during the epoch which terminated in the publication of the Greek Gospels, may apply the same principle to the writings of Josephus, and declare them annulled by these unique productions; and the success of the imposition hitherto may embolden some one to make the attempt. No saying; but the general heart of the world is sound, and no one need expect again to gain its ear for any philosophy that does not root itself in facts and derive itself therefrom by rigour of logic. These records of Josephus cannot be abolished, because he is "the most learned, the most accurate, and the most unprejudiced historian, not only of the Jewish affairs, but of whatever he has written upon; and this has been his character from the first publication of his writings through the several centuries down to the present."

How, then, are we to reconcile the traditional account of the Pontius Pilate prophet, published so many years *after*, with the historical account given of the same personage by Josephus? Shall we set off the traditional writers against Josephus as equally able, "most learned, most accurate, and most unprejudiced"? or shall we cast them aside as the most unlearned, the most inaccurate, and the most prejudiced, having in view the propagation of a new philosophy and the formation of a new religious sect, under the perverting power of which they could see in the faith of the Jewish race and the facts of their history only an echo and response to their own groundless phantasies?

It has been our sad task to show how often the four Greek writers blend events and characters which can only be disintegrated by research into the facts of history. A further instance occurs in confirmation of the charge in connection with the deaths of the two Herods—that of Herod the first, "who was eaten up of worms," and that of his grandson, Agrippa the Great, both described by the historian. This is his relation of the latter event: *—

"Now when Agrippa had reigned three years over all Judea, he came to the city Cæsarea, which was formerly called Strato's Tower, and there he exhibited shows in honour of Cæsar, upon his being informed that there was a certain festival celebrated to make vows for his safety. At which festival a great multitude was gotten together of the principal persons, and such as were of dignity through his province. On the second day of which shows he put on a garment made wholly of silver, and of a contexture truly wonderful, and came into the theatre early in the morning; at which time the silver of his garment, being illuminated by the first reflection of the sun's rays upon it, shone out after a surprising manner, and was so resplendent as to spread a horror over those that looked intently upon him; and presently his flatterers cried out, one from one place and another from another (though not for his good),

* "Antiquities," Book xix. chap. 8, sec. 2.

that he was a god; and they added, 'Be thou merciful to us; for although we have hitherto reverenced thee only as a man, yet shall we henceforth own thee as superior to mortal nature.' Upon this the king did neither rebuke them nor reject their impious flattery; but as he presently afterwards looked up, he saw an owl sitting on a certain rope over his head, and immediately understood that this bird was the messenger of ill tidings, as it had once been the messenger of good tidings to him, and fell into the deepest sorrow. A severe pain also arose in his belly and began in a most violent manner. He therefore looked upon his friends, and said, 'I whom you call a god am commanded presently to depart this life, while Providence thus reproves the lying words you just now said to me; and I, who was by you called immortal, am immediately to be hurried away by death. But I am bound to accept of what Providence allots, as it pleases God; for we have by no means lived ill, but in a splendid and happy manner.' When he said this, his pain was become violent. Accordingly he was carried into the palace, and the rumour went abroad everywhere that he would certainly die in a little time."

In conclusion, Josephus continues:—

"When he had been quite worn out by the pain in his belly for five days, he departed this life, being in the fifty-fourth year of his age and the seventh year of his reign."

Our readers will observe that this account of the death of Agrippa the Great, the grandson of the first Herod, is a separate and different account from that of the death of his grandfather many years previously; and the following quotation from the Acts shows that the traditional accounts have blended into one the deaths of the grandfather and the grandson :—

"And upon a set day *Herod*, arrayed in royal apparel, sat upon his throne, and made an oration unto them. And the people gave a shout, saying, It is the voice of a god, and not of a man. And immediately the angel of the Lord smote him, because he gave not God the glory; and he was eaten up of worms, and gave up the ghost" (Acts xii. 21, 22).

In this version an angel of the Lord is introduced, instead of the owl seen by the king in the historian's account, agreeably to a style these writers have of representing calamities that overtake the persecutors of their faith as special judgments from the Lord in their behalf. But apart from the false idea thus conveyed in regard to the interposition of Providence, the facts are jumbled in the usual way, and the same reckless disregard appears of the sacredness of history. Not content with the dramatic effect of a picture in which death with his terrors comes upon the scene to humble the glory of a king and give the lie to the fulsome flattery of his courtiers, they must substitute an angel for an owl as the special minister of vengeance. To these writers one Herod is as good as another, and it does not matter how they distort the facts, if they can only throw them into a form which will invest with awe and mystery their own vain philosophy. Now, however, that this trick is being brought to light, the facts will be sundered and set in their proper place by the light of history.

We have separated the Pontius Pilate pretender from all connection with the Jesus of the Gospels, the meek Jesus of Jerusalem from the Galilean Jesus of the sword, the death of Herod the Great from that of his grandson Agrippa, and we have referred the doctrine of the immortality of the soul to the early Jewish sects, and the gospel which first preached the kingdom of God to Judas of Galilee. The origin of that communism which surrendered the right to private possessions for the benefit of the community is due, as we have seen, to the sect of the Essenes. The light in the heavens and the miraculous opening of the great gate, reported in connection with the imprisonment of Simon Peter, are proved to have taken place in the time of the historical Jesus. The birth on a Passover of a lamb from a heifer in the stables of the Temple, which had been brought there to be offered in sacrifice for the sins of the people, and the star that appeared in the heavens above the house at about the same time, together with other supernatural manifestations, are evidently the basis of certain well-known traditions in the Gospel story.

It is known to be a fact that Herodias had but one daughter by her first husband, named Salome, who was married to her uncle Philip, who, dying a year and a half before Tiberias, left her a widow; and yet she is called a damsel by the Greek writers, who represent her as asking her stepfather for the head of John the Baptist, and that during the lifetime of her husband, the matter being reported, as usual, in reckless disregard of the facts. Neither is there any historical evidence of a person existing at the time answering to the character of John. The baptist Banus, who is the only historical personage mentioned by Josephus as having any connection with the symbolical use of water, must have been a comparatively young man to have gained the reputation he enjoyed when Josephus was his disciple. He was, no doubt, the original John, born therefore at the time Luke says Jesus was. Had Banus had a predecessor in the same line of the name of John, he would not have failed to mention it to Josephus when he stayed with him, and Josephus would not have failed to record what he heard, interested as he was to leave behind him, as the main labour of his life, a record of the religious movements of his time and country. Moreover, if the appearance of this John was such as to leave an impression on the human race a century and a half after he was dead, is it not evident that he must have made a greater on the men of his own generation, and most of all on the man who was so quick to remark less significant phenomena, among the rest, the ascetic life of this very Banus? Is there not, therefore, every reason to presume that this Banus is the Baptist connected with the anachronous traditional Jesus? If the Evangelists have been misled as to the date of the one, it is reasonable to conclude that they have been so with regard to that of the other.

Now all this, taken in connection with the proved historical untrustworthiness of the traditional accounts, points to but one conclusion, and that is that the accounts given by Josephus of the Pontius Pilate pretender, of Banus, and of the two Jesuses—the appearance of which last was accompanied by portents without precedent in merely secular history—form the basis of the story of the characters and events that figure on the page of the traditional narratives, otherwise this last is a purely mythical invention and without any historical groundwork whatever.

But can the narrative of the four Greek writers, composed long after the fall of Jerusalem, be only a *myth?* To this question a negative reply must be given, apart altogether from the demonstration in disproof derived from history, as whatever inaccuracies abound in the relation, it is *a priori* inconceivable how a story *prima facie* historical could have arisen without a historical basis. For the facts do not first bring to light a philosophy previously unknown; these are only collected together in a personal form from far and near as embodiments of its principles. The novelty lies in the composition of the facts as embodiments of the principles, not in the principles themselves as so embodied. The narrative reports, and not unskilfully localises, a jumble of historical events, extending from before the founding of the Jewish state to the fall of Jerusalem, as illustrating a foregone theosophy, and is no myth, but the reflection of a real movement of a section of the Jewish mind before and after the national dissolution and dispersion. No doubt other elements, having more or less a historical root, were added. The strife which goes on between good and evil in the soul of man and under the providence of God had come to be regarded under Parsee teaching as a contest between the angels of light and darkness. The doctrine of the incarnation, or God manifest in the flesh, had been wafted thither from the banks of the Ganges. "In the Sanskrit dictionary, compiled more than two thousand years ago," says Sir William Jones, "we have the whole history of the incarnate deity, Krishna, born of a virgin and miraculously escaping in his infancy from the reigning tyrant of the country, Cama. And not only in books are these mythic tales recorded, but in the less perishable memorials of the old rock temples. One of the rock temples at Matthura is built in the form of a cross, and contains within a statue of *Krishna, the saviour of men.*" We know where the communism of the primitive Christians came from, and the doctrine of the immortality of the soul was common to all the sects of the Jews, except the Sadducees. The incidents of the life of Jesus we have shown meet in the lives of the two Jesuses and those of others of their contemporaries; and the doctrine of the unity of God is a legacy from the Bible. From sources such as these the philosophy came, of which the medley of facts put together in the traditional narrative was regarded as the embodiment; and this it has been since necessary to support with the subtlety of sophistical argument, and to enforce with the terror of excommunication, affecting at once the life that now is and that which is to come hereafter.

The law must be obeyed when exacted by the fanaticism of bigotry and enforced at the fire of the stake. Heresy could not be tolerated in Christendom, seeing it subverted the civil rights of nations. The present Christian populations of Europe and America are the children of their parents, bound, in the interest of their civil privileges, to uphold the dogmas and institutions of the Church. The institutions of ages, inwoven as they are into the framework of society, are not to be uprooted in a day. A sacred oath has been exacted for centuries from the sovereigns of England, pledging them to defend the Christian faith, as on the maintenance of that faith, it is thought, depends the permanency of the constitution of the country. The subjects are individually free, but the ruling power is enslaved, because it is presumed that if the monarchy should cease to be Christian, the glory of England would pass away. Loyal-hearted as this country is, it still distrusts the naked truth ungarnished by fiction, though there are signs of the dawn of a day not far off when the English nation, partly in quest of, partly driven on, the eternal rocks, may plant the throne of its power on their adamantine basis.

When we have enumerated the sources from which the heterogeneous principles of Christianity are obtained, we shall find we have almost completed the catalogue of its peculiarities. Much, if not all, of a historical nature will be found in Josephus; much of the doctrine, perverted and misapplied, is imported from the Bible, while the Lord's Prayer, as it is termed, and the parables of Jesus, are plagiarisms from the Talmud.

We cannot illustrate this serious charge better than by quoting a few passages from the able pen of Bethune English, author of the "Grounds of Christianity Examined," a book which well deserves the regard of the student of truth clearly, logically, and conclusively demonstrated. At chap. v. p. 22 of his work he remarks:—

"But since one would esteem it almost incredible that the Apostles could persuade men to believe Jesus to be the Messiah, unless they had at least some proof to offer to their conviction, let us consider and examine the proofs adduced by the Apostles and their followers from the Old Testament for that purpose.

"Of the strength or weakness of the proofs for Christianity out of the Old Testament we are well qualified to judge, as we have the Old and New Testaments in our hands, the first containing what are offered as proofs of Christianity, and the latter the application of those proofs; and we should seem to have nothing more to do but to compare the Old and New Testaments together.

"But then these proofs taken out of the Old Testament and urged in the New, being sometimes not to be found in the Old, nor urged in the New according to the literal and obvious sense which they appear to have in their supposed places in the Old, and therefore not proofs according to the rules of interpretation established by reason, and acted upon in interpreting every other ancient book, almost all

Christian commentators in the Bible and advocates for the religion of the New Testament, both ancient and modern, have judged them to be applied in a secondary or typical, or mystical or allegorical, or enigmatical sense ; that is, in a sense different from the obvious and literal sense which they bear in the Old Testament.

"Thus, for example, Matthew, after having given an account of the conception of Mary and the birth of Jesus, says in chap. i. 22, 23, ' All this was done that it might be fulfilled which was spoken by the prophet, saying, Behold a virgin shall be with child, and shall bring forth a son, and they shall call his name Immanuel.' But the words as they stand in Isa. vii. 14, from whence they are taken, do in their obvious and literal sense relate to a young woman in the days of Ahaz, king of Judah, as will appear, if we consider the context.

" When Rezin, king of Syria, and Pekah, king of Israel, were confederates in arms together against Ahaz, king of Judah, Isaiah the prophet was sent by God, first to comfort Ahaz and the nation, and then to assure them by a sign that his enemies should in a little time be confounded. But Ahaz, refusing a sign at the prophet's hands, the prophet said (see the passage), ' The Lord shall give you a sign : behold a virgin, or young woman ' (for the Hebrew word means *both*, as the Jews maintained in the primitive ages against the Christians, and as is now acknowledged and established beyond dispute by the best Hebrew scholars of this age) ' shall conceive, and bear a son, and shall call his name Immanuel. Butter and honey shall he eat, that he may know to refuse the evil and choose the good. For before the child shall know to refuse the evil and choose the good, the land which thou abhorrest shall be forsaken of both her kings.' And this sign is accordingly given Ahaz by the prophet, who, chap.

viii. 2, 18, took two witnesses and went to the said young woman, who in due time conceived and bare a son, after whose birth the projects of Rezin and Pekah were, it appears, soon confounded, according to the prophecy and sign given by the prophet."

And the prophet himself puts it beyond dispute that this is the proper interpretation of the prophecy, as well by *express words* as by his whole narrative; for he adds, "Behold I and the children whom the Lord hath given me are for signs and for wonders in Israel from the Lord of hosts, that dwelleth in Mount Zion." This is the plain sense of the prophet in the passage, and he is so understood by one of the most judicious of interpreters, the great Grotius. Indeed, to suppose the prophet as having in view the conception of Mary, and the birth of a son from her as a virgin, is an utter absurdity, and contrary to the very intent and design of the sign given by the prophet, which was to be an evidence to satisfy Ahaz that the message of the prophet respecting the two kings coming against him was from the Lord; and this it could not be, if it referred to an event that was to happen seven hundred years afterwards. That were as if the prophet had said, "Before the child born *seven hundred years hence* shall distinguish between good and evil, the land which thou abhorrest shall be forsaken by both her kings;" which might be a piece of banter, but could be no sign.

We need not go over the arguments, now so stale, in evidence of the misquotations in which the Evangelists indulge to support the allegation of the Messiahship of Jesus. Enough has been written on that point to satisfy all but the most bigotedly orthodox. And yet the vindication of the reference is not faith in Christ, who wrote nothing; it is only faith in four obscure writers, who are contradicted by the Bible, contradicted by history, contradicted by their ancestors, contradicted by their contemporaries, contradicted by themselves, and contradicted by one another. No faith can be placed in such writings. Never, either in works of controversy or in the courts of justice, is any reliance placed on the asseverations of persons who stand convicted of untruth and unreason, albeit it is to the statements of these four men that the Church compels obedience, and the body of the people yield submission. Under faith in them the most opposite philosophies have shaken hands together, and thereby the whole affairs of the nations have been thrown into confusion and distraction. That faith has filled Europe with bloodshed and rancour for eighteen centuries, and now, by resolution into its original elements, it is filling the world with contending sects and parties of all shades of contradictory opinion.

It is not possible, we think, for any reasonable person, after careful research, to maintain any longer the mythical derivation of the Gospel narrative. It is simply an *olla podrida*, or heterogeneous *mélange* of ancient philosophies and historical facts, so that all schools and sects can pick out of the mess what may please their several tastes and appetites. Each contends with the other for the honour of its support, and all manner of subtle shifts are resorted to to make it blow hot and cold on the same subject. There is no point on which it cannot be brought into court, either for justification or condemnation, and no party whose interests it cannot be quoted to serve.

CHAPTER XVI.

The opposite qualities in the character of Christ due to the mingling of two characters, not two natures—Perversions of Messianic predictions—Pious frauds—Questionable theology, morality, and spirituality—The beginnings of Christianity.

No character that has been handed down to us by history, whether sacred or secular, is to be compared for gentleness and divine zeal with that of the meek Jesus of Josephus and the God-man of the Gospels. Both these, as they were one in spirit and passion, so they were identical, and are proved to be one in the words they uttered as well as the events of their lives. Both predicted the downfall of their country and their own fateful death; both lived by the ministry of others, and suffered persecution and martyrdom at the hands of the State; both were publicly mocked and scorned and tortured, and cherished no revengeful feeling towards their enemies in their heart; and both raised their warning voice in all corners of Judea, and displayed a fervour which other men reckoned mad. Here, however, the proof of the identification stops, for other elements appear in the character of the traditional Jesus referable to a different historical root. And as he resembles the meek Jesus in his gentleness, so he resembles his namesake the Galilean Jesus in fiery temper and severity; and the identity in this case, as in the other, is proved, as we have shown, by a parallelism in the history as well as a parallelism in the spirit of the life. The features which characterise and the incidents that befall the traditional Jesus are explicable by reference now to the one, now to the other, of these historical figures, the fault in the character being due entirely to the preponderance of the severe over the softer nature, so that the historical man is less faulty than the traditional God.

It is the business of the critic to show where the one character steps to the front and the other retires to the background. We may be sure it is the severe Jesus who speaks when he requires a man to sacrifice his natural affection and leave his dead father unburied. It is not the meek one, but the severe, who urges his followers to refer their cause to the arbitration of the sword, and who was arraigned as a malefactor. It is the latter, not the former, who boasts that his gospel would divide not only man from man, but kinsman from kinsman, so that "a man's foes should be those of his own household." Not the meek one, but the severe, complains of the desertion of his relatives and friends, still more of being forsaken by the God who looks with compassion on all His children. Nor is it the meek one, but the severe, who, in scorn of the sacred order of the world, makes himself the friend of publicans and sinners, and who accepts the homage of worship that is paid him by people of uncertain character. There is a pathetic element in the traditional Jesus that has rendered the Christian world insensible to the harsher and less lovable features in the picture; and it was the sympathy with which the fate of the meek Jesus could not fail to be regarded that naturally contributed to invest his name with that halo of divinity which in the traditional report eventually dominated and overshone every other quality.

Against the meek historical Jesus no word of reproach could be raised in his lifetime, still less after his sorrowful decease, and no one can read his tragic history to-day without a sentiment of sadness at his fate. The divine passion ascribed to him by the historian is affirmed of no other figure in the history of the period, and no other could by possibility develop into the conception of the traditional Christ. It is this one whom the tradition has mistakingly confounded with the pretended prophet slain by Pilate, and it is because he did not deserve, as it seemed, such treatment that the Jesus of tradition has called forth the sympathy and commanded the homage of so many of our race.

It lay in the nature of the case that the inconsistent features in the portrait should remain unrecognised in the prostrate admiration which could regard only its nobler side; and this is the sole reason why the analysis we are attempting has never till now been made. His instincts were so generous, his sacrifices so great, and his aim so exalted, that it seemed impiety to hint, still more single out, any fault. A character so holy in the estimation of his followers, could not utter or exact anything unjust and so it was concluded that whatever he might say and require was right. Jesus might judge mankind, but mankind may not judge him; he spoke, it was thought, from a higher platform and more advanced than it is given to any mortal to reach. But when, rid of our superstitions, we dare to analyse his character, we observe a mixture of the base with the precious, which, like the clay and the iron in the prophet's image, will not *unite*. The holier the character, the less seemly is the combination, the more reason there is to question it, and the greater the obligation to trace it out. What we look for in one we can worship is integrity and not incoherence, a character moulded after some such pattern as that commended to us in Holy Writ; conceived, that is, in the fear of God and developed in brotherly love. Whatever is not consistently devout and human in affection and action should be cast into the fire and as dross purged out.

Thus far, then, we think we are warranted to go. While we may not criticise aught within a sphere we are forbidden to enter, or where, if we enter it, we may only worship, and with veiled face, we may and must pronounce judgment on what outside of that sphere challenges our homage, and, as even Christianity itself exhorts, " try the spirits whether they be of God." And if this is our general duty, it is still more our duty in regard to him who claims, as Christ does, our entire and absolute confidence. And this we are bold enough to maintain in regard to him, that there are actions and utterances ascribed to him which are foreign to the nobler side of his nature, such as neither call forth our admiration nor provoke us to follow in his steps. It is no doubt difficult to unriddle the mazes of such a character, owing to the contradiction there often is among his sayings, and between what he says and what he does, due, as we have seen, to the blending of the meek with the violent Galilean Jesus.

Now it is surely the most sacred duty of a son to perform the last office due to a dead parent; and yet we see Jesus scorning this sentiment of humanity, and saying to one who pleads this duty, "Let the dead bury their dead." Can such a statement suggest itself in a humane bosom? Is it entitled to the respect of human hearts? Again, what sort of a morality is that which Jesus enforces when he requires of his followers to shake off from their feet the dust of an inhospitable city, and pronounces over that city a woe more terrible than that which overtook the Cities of the Plain? And what shall we say of one who, when the occasion called for simple moral courage, bade his disciples sell their garments and buy swords? Whoso can accept such teaching as divine teaching, can accept anything; and the fact that so many do is only one symptom more of the prostration of intellect exacted and enforced by the Christian system. Yet how some men can accept such teaching as divine, and persuade themselves into the practicability of a morality so inconsistent, passes belief. The morality that encourages the use of the sword against recognised authority could never proceed from the same lips as those which pronounced the meek blessed; nor could the followers of Jesus, who had renounced the rights of property, give of their own to buy anything. This morality exactly suits, not the character of the meek martyr, but the man of violence, accompanied by an armed following, prone without urging, like Peter, to avenge itself by an act of force.

We meet with no other Jesuses in history than those two mentioned as, in their combination, constituting the character of the Jesus of tradition given in the Gospels; and it is the fact of this derivation of the latter from these two which accounts for the moral inconsistencies in the traditional accounts. It is probable the amalgamation would have been suggested or discovered long ago but for the hypothesis, invented at an early date, and soon accepted as a fact, of the union in the person of Jesus of the deity with humanity. And, in fact, this theory, adopted as an article of the Christian creed, has been adduced to explain the inconsistencies referred to, and the explanation has been received as satisfactory by the general Christian mind. And indeed this theory is more than the assertion of a union between the two natures; in it the human is cast aside or merged, and only deity speaks and acts.

Now, in regard to this theory, which is entirely

opposed to our philosophy, we maintain that, despite the acceptance it has had, and the length of time it has stood its ground, it has only a speculative basis, and no solid foundation in fact. All which the facts warrant is the assertion of the combination into one of two opposite human natures, as these separately appeared in the actual recorded history of two contemporaries of the same name. The Christian theory of the two natures rests on a less secure basis. Nor let any one object that we characterise such a doctrine as a mere theory. That is a term usually applied to what has some show of reason in its favour, while this and many other Christian dogmas have not so much as that, being inconsistent alike with reason and truth, and unable to stand even the contact of rational criticism. Is it, for example, not enough to shock the first principles of reason and truth to affirm that the Messianic prophecies foretell the advent of an earthly king, and maintain that these prophecies have had their fulfilment in the advent of no mere earthly king, but of God Himself? Is not this to cast away the very premises upon which the idea of the Messiah rests? For the prophecies that predicted his coming and gave rise to the expectation, not only do not reveal that the Messiah would be God, but in plainest terms promise the reverse. So that we see in this instance the Christian philosophy denies its own premises in pretending to be a fulfilment of prophecies of which it is the contradiction, utter and complete.

It is an outrage on common sense, and an assertion begotten of pure unreason, to argue for a system which announces that Messiah is God by appealing to prophecies which predict the advent of a king of a mere earthly line. And what force of reason is there in maintaining and believing that the prophecies which promise a Messiah in the latter days have been fulfilled in the appearance of a prophet eighteen hundred years ago? Who does not see that, if the Messiah appeared then, these prophecies are not true? And if these are not true, how vain is it to appeal to them in evidence! Then what ground is there other than a speculative one, and that most impious, for the assertion that this Messiah who proclaimed the advent of these latter days is Almighty God? Could He be deceived? Could He deceive? What other ground is there than a speculative one for believing in writings as divine that can make such asseverations as these, and dare implicate the Deity and His so-called representative in their delusions and deceits? Then, again, how unscrupulous it is to make the Messiah plead for himself on the ground that Elias, who was promised to precede him, had come in the person of John, his own cousin, who, however he might represent another, was not he! Has not such an argument as this, to say the least of it, a most disingenuous look? It is as much as to say that an appearance promised was fulfilled in an appearance not promised. But, indeed, why enlarge? Sophistries of this quality in these narratives appear quite limitless, and a bare enumeration of the fallacies to which the writers of them resort in defence of this cardinal doctrine would fill a volume.

What, now, are we to think of the morality which fabricates such statements? Is it a wicked or virtuous act to propagate falsehood? To our mind the propagation of such falsehoods, referring, as in this case, to serious matters, is far more heinous than when the subject is insignificant. We do not believe that pious frauds are at all pious, but that they are most impious and deserve utter reprobation. They have helped the cause of confusion, and not of order, by propping up superstitions that have no other foundation. And that the philosophy which these frauds are invented to support is without support in reason, is evident. Take, for instance, this postulate, implied in the logic adopted: that principles received as truth when combined are to be rejected as untruths when separated. The doctrine, for example, of the unity of God, accepted in its pure simplicity, though taught, and as such enforced, under penalties by God Himself, is not true except in union with the opposite doctrine of the Trinity, and the worship of either without the other is treated as idolatry. The Deity is one and *indivisible;* but if you do not worship each *part* of the Deity, and there are three parts—God the Father, God the Son, and God the Holy Ghost— *woe be unto thee.* There is only *one Deity*, and He must have your *undivided worship;* but if you worship *one only*, without dividing your worship with two other beings, *woe, woe unto thee*.

Thus, too, the doctrine of the two principles of Light and Darkness is false in the lips of a Persian prophet but true in the mouth of Paul, though it was not his, but a plagiarism from the Parsee religion. So also the doctrine which regards *Krishna*, the saviour of men, as an incarnate God; and the doctrines of the resurrection and of the immortality of the soul, both of which are ethnic beliefs, are of no account separately, but become factors in a revelation from Heaven when once blended into the harmonies of the Christian faith! Separately these beliefs are the assertions of opposing philosophies; only when combined into a self-contradictory whole, do they constitute a religion worthy of belief! It verily needs all the sophistry human genius can devise to fabricate arguments to render plausible a philosophy such as this.

If we inquire, we shall find that this philosophy is contradicted by theology, by metaphysics, by history, and the character of the evidences adduced in proof.

It sets itself in opposition to the theology of the Bible, and, while professing to rest upon it, really undermines it. It does not indeed accuse that holy book of propagating false ideas, but it declares that its laws and ordinances were temporary, and have been abolished under the new dispensation. In abolishing these, it abrogates laws and commandments which itself admits emanated from the Creator for the guidance of man. It appears, as is explained, however, that there was a duration clause, limiting the operation of these, which, though unproclaimed at the time, was announced when a new dispensation was inaugurated, which clause virtually falsifies the old (for that asserts itself as absolutely and eternally true), and accuses the Divine Being, as we argued before, both of *suppressio veri* and *suggestio falsi*; for the new dispensation gives to the world a rival God, who yet is no God, for he is to render his power back again into the hands of the only living and true God, that "He may be all in all." Language like this implies that God is not all in all at present, while the rival God reigns; and if God be not all in all under this new state of things, how can it be maintained that Jesus is God? Jesus is not God if God be not all in all now, simply because he is in power. And if Jesus were *God* and *reigned* in heaven, would not God now be all in all? The plain inference from all this is, that God is not all in all now, because the Jesus of the Christians has usurped His place—because, in other words, the Christian theology makes man God.

Anyhow, the distinction drawn by Paul on this point between the reign of Jesus and the reign of God is a virtual denial of the equality of the former with the latter, *i.e.*, of the deity of Jesus Christ; yet the Christian religion requires the worship of Jesus, contrary to the spirit of the commandment, which proclaims God to be a jealous God, who will not share His glory with any other; for is not Jesus, by confession of the Christian apologists themselves, another being?

The thesis maintained, indeed, is that Jesus is God, and should be worshipped as God; but it is not denied by those who advance this theory that he is another being, and that the worship of any other being than the Creator is an infringement of the Creator's command. A likeness surely is different from Himself, and to set up a likeness is expressly forbidden; yet Paul describes Jesus as the image of God, and, in express contradiction to the command, exacts for that image the worship that is to be reserved for God Himself. And indeed the Christian writings throughout, while they claim for Jesus the worship due to deity, make use of expressions which imply that he is not God. A corporeal being cannot be the image of the incorporeal. If the seed of David now reigns in heaven, he must be a corporeal king, and the kingdom is not universal if the king is one day to lapse again into a subject. In such fashion do these writings belie their own assertions, and convict themselves of setting aside, by their traditions, the commandments of God.

It is St. Paul who offends most in emitting these contradictory assertions, speaking of Jesus at once as God and as another than God. But then it is to be remembered that it was he who, in contradiction of all he has written, solemnly protested that he had never said aught against the Temple or the Jewish faith. Thus he pleads in Acts xxiv. 11-13:—

"Because that thou mayest understand that there are yet but twelve days since I went up to Jerusalem for to worship. And they neither found me in the Temple disputing with any man, neither raising up the people, neither in the synagogues nor in the city. Neither can they prove the things whereof they now accuse me." As if the whole industry of that Apostle was not bent on demolishing just those very institutions which he here tries to persuade his hearers he upholds! But indeed it is the very nature of Christianity to pervert the moral character, and to exalt those into saintship who do not even speak truth. All the associates of Jesus, when brought before the bar of just criticism, are more or less deficient in moral character, and those whom he condemns exhibit a loftier *morale* than those whom he loves and exalts. The young man who would have shared his possessions with the poor and needy is told that it is harder for rich men to enter heaven than for a camel to pass through a needle's eye. And yet there is no nobler virtue than charity, and no greater outrage could be perpetrated against religion and morality than to make incarnate deity exclude those who possessed it from the kingdom of God. Verily those who seriously believe that God Himself has put His ban on the philanthropy of riches are likely to believe, and say, and do a great many unaccountable things.

Accordingly, it need not surprise us to hear the author of this morality declare his preference for mean and worthless people over the pure and generous, and preach a gospel of forgiveness which throws open the kingdom of heaven to the one, while it excludes the other.

Here, however, is one true oracle which is put into the prophet's lips (Matt. xx. 16, 17) :—" And behold one came and said unto him, Good master, what good thing shall I do that I may have eternal life ? And he said unto him, Why callest thou me good ? There is none good but one, that is, God; but if thou wilt enter into life, keep the commandments." In no stronger words could he disclaim at once the divinity and the perfection which his disciples ascribe to him ; and than his own no more decisive testimony, one would think, could be brought into court. How then can any one maintain either of these dogmas in the face of this repudiation from his own lips ? No sophistry can reconcile them with this declaration; and yet the theologian who believes them is bound to make the attempt. Here is what Canon Liddon says on the point, at p. 367 in the " Bampton Lectures " for 1866, on the " Divinity of our Lord and Saviour Jesus Christ." Speaking of Jesus, he says, " He welcomes by a tacit approval this profound homage of which he is the object. His rebuke to the rich young man implies, not that he himself had no real claim to be called ' Good Master,' but that such a title, in the mouth of the person before him, was an unmeaning compliment."

To such shifts of sophistry does an eminent scholar and gifted divine, who is well able to estimate the exact value of language and draw the legitimate deductions therefrom, resort in parrying an argument that tells against a cherished dogma. In his enthusiasm for the cause he advocates, he loses sight of what is due to, and worthy of, the character of him whom he pleads for as the Creator of the world. In his desire to prove him God he proves him less, and as not entitled to the credit of being regarded even as an ingenuous man. He makes Jesus affect not to be what he is, and say he is not good and not God, when he is both; and this he affects with one who, so far from being an unintelligent worshipper, is worthy to be taught that, if he would enter into life, he must keep the commandments. But even supposing Canon Liddon is right in his deduction—and for argument's sake we may admit he is—the conception that the Divine Being would condescend so to deny Himself, implies an idea of Him which, if applied to a good man, would not fail to provoke just indignation.

Even admitting, however, as all Christians should, that Jesus meant what he asserted, and declined the proffered homage as not due, the dilemma is not at all lessened, inasmuch as Jesus at other times avows himself to be God; so that one is tempted to exclaim, "What kind of a God is this, who at one time stakes the salvation of mankind on faith in his divinity, and at another repudiates even the title to be called good, and therefore to be called divine?" Surely those who respect him should not condemn us if we take him at his word, and refuse to believe that he who says he is both divine and not divine can be God. Greater reason have we to deny his godhead than others have to affirm it, for he proves himself not to be divine in at one time claiming and at another disclaiming that he is God; for neither Jesus nor any other being who is in such bewilderment about himself can be the Divine Being. The God of the four Greek writers and of Paul is not a being that can be regarded in such a light, neither can he be looked upon as the consistent declarer of truth, wisdom, or goodness.

It has been the fashion for ages to accept a contrary estimate of his character, and load his name with an enthusiastic laudation that is not borne out by facts. The God of the four Greek writers is lowered to the level of man, while the man they endeavour to exalt is not elevated either in sentiment or deed to the level of God. Man has not been elevated by this belief to be equal to the Deity, while the idea of Deity has been brought as low as, if not lower than, the idea of man. Hence we find attributes of the lowest type ascribed to Jesus even by those who seek to exalt him.

The assumption of the sophists, that Christianity is in point of spirituality superior to the materialistic monotheism of the Jews, proves on examination not only to be not true, but the reverse of true. Spirituality is applicable to those only who worship the spiritual, and materialism is chargeable against those who combine the worship of a mortal with that of the

Immortal. The religion of the one is pure, unadulterated spirituality; the other is a materialism, all the more gross that it has supplanted a more spiritual worship. The worship of the spirit alone, unless blended with this worship of humanity, forsooth, entails only perdition! while the worship of humanity combined with that of spirituality will entitle the worshipper to eternal salvation! What is it that Christianity most worships? The spiritual worship is of no avail, or worse, when uncombined with materialistic devotion. Upon close examination, it will be found that a false idea has taken possession of every part of the Christian system. The result is that that system has been regarded as supernaturally begotten, and those who accept it are entirely intolerant of adverse criticism, however impartial. Under these circumstances, those trained up in it have been taught from childhood to regard its claims from only one point of view, to the exclusion of every other phase of the question; and in this way reason and wisdom, when brought into conflict with it, are brought face to face with a power that has no *scientific frontier* and no defensive works, and cannot logically hold one post against the forces of such assailants. With a civil war for ever raging within—for each tenet is in conflict with the others—it would not hold out for a day, but for the sophistry, bigotry, and denunciation so closely leagued with it; these forces, when allied, are, from the superstitions they engender, not easily conquered; and it is this unholy alliance which has been the mainstay of the great delusion. Thousands of sermons every Sunday, and books without number, more or less impregnated with Christian sentiment, are listened to or read by hundreds of thousands with approving sympathy, while a book convincingly proving that the foundation of the whole structure is a mass of loose sand, and which will carry conviction in the future, would lie unnoticed on our library shelves.

The ultimate test of the claims of any pretender to godhead is his power to prove that his pretensions are good. It is not the power of fulminating denunciations against unbelievers, nor threats against them of eternal perdition, for these are human devices and not divine, unless accompanied by proofs that the message they enforce is a heavenly message, and that it is an utterance, perhaps an inspired one, direct from the heart of man. The threats and denunciations uttered in the interest of Christianity, it is alleged, however, come from the lips of the Eternal God, from which nothing unwise or untruthful can proceed. The deeds, sentiments, and characters so inspired must needs be of a sublime nature, such as to satisfy the entire race, and exert an influence never to be effaced. And yet the influence of Jesus has only been impressed upon a portion of mankind, and that posthumously, not contemporaneously, his fame, contrary to all experience, growing brighter with increasing distance of time; for experience teaches that with time all lights grow paler, and all glories wax dimmer, unless you feed them with fresh fuel or kindle them with fresh fire.

Can it be that the Eternal visited the earth in the form of a man, performing public miracles so wonderful as to have had no precedent since the world began, and that mankind did not at the time take the slightest notice either of Him or His deeds, preferring to record instead incidents of the period not at all wonderful, as if a conspiracy had been formed to throw a veil over His public manifestations and acts as wonderful as themselves? What! Pontius Pilate, and Josephus, and Justus the Elder, and Pliny, and Seneca, to combine with the rest of the world to ignore the appearance of this mighty, nay, Almighty One, who, amongst other proofs of his presence, drew signs from heaven, signs from the earth, and signs from under the earth, by bringing the dead to life, observable to all, and whose healing virtue was such that it was felt by those who but touched his garment! Could all these things have been kept a secret so as to deprive immediate posterity of the knowledge of them? Is it credible that all mankind could have been kept in the dark in the very presence of so shining a light? of one too, who had so many followers, and these followers endowed with powers as miraculous as himself, and that they determined the world should know what the world knew already, and have proof of what the world had proof already, and not forget what the world forgot? And these followers could not but know what Josephus had written respecting the pretender who deluded the people and was killed by Pontius Pilate. Why did they not controvert this statement of Josephus, who gave proof of the truth of his version by appealing to well-known historical transactions? Did these followers ever record the facts? If so, there is no relic of their records except a traditional one, composed later on, when all the contemporaries of the period had gone to their rest. In the middle of the second century we find a record, according to what, with a certain limited number, was already a crystallised belief, which, had it been crystallised earlier, would have been published earlier.

The career of the meek historical Jesus of Josephus must, in consideration of their disbelief of his warnings and in sorrow over his tragic fate, have powerfully arrested the thoughtful regards of his immediate posterity, and strongly tempted many to collect and publish his history as a monition to the other nations of the earth. The impression he made must have been, by the awful circumstances of his life, of a most dramatic and indelible character, after the truth of his prophecies had been realised, when the glorious Temple was now in ashes, when the great city Jerusalem, the Holy City, had become a ruin, and the few that were spared from fire, sword, and pestilence were scattered to the "four winds," to wander about homeless over the face of the earth. What Jew with any regard for the land and faith of his fathers could look back upon that dire catastrophe without mixing up the memory of it with the memory of him who for seven years and five months had in such loud wail and sore martyrdom foretold the woe and desolation that had come upon them, and who seemed to have disappeared Elijah-like in a chariot of the fire that had been kindled? Is it to be wondered at that there should be some who imagined a new dispensation had begun when God had visited the nation with such a curse? Could any one after that believe that they were the chosen race of the Highest, and the religion they professed a light for all the race.

It was of no avail to plead that the Jewish religion was of divine institution, and that the curse had come, not because it was false, but because, as it threatened itself, the nation had become unfaithful. The world who looked on saw in the events that had happened the signs of a faith that had fallen obsolete and the promise of a new order, which some affected had been uttered by the Jesus of the dissolution, who was at first regarded as the prophet and finally as the Son of God. The tradition of his general character as one instinct with a "divine fury," and the wonderful events connected with his decease, such as the mysterious light at the Passover, the opening of the great gate of the city, the provision of the miraculous lamb for sacrifice, as if it were the last that would be needed, and the quaking and sounds at Pentecost, all contributed to impart a divine significance to his appearance, and to give plausibility to the assumption that the Jewish era had closed and a new one begun. Only here is the hitch; how could such things come to be affirmed of the Pontius Pilate pretender, who, according to Luke's chronology, must have been but a stripling in years? and how could events which happened thirty years later in reference to another be ascribed to his time and him? And how could he have uttered those words put into his mouth by St. Matthew if he had suffered in Pontius Pilate's reign? (Matt. xxiii. 32-36):—

"Fill ye up then the measure of your fathers. Ye serpents, ye generation of vipers, how can ye escape the damnation of hell? Wherefore, behold, I send unto you prophets, and wise men, and scribes; and some of them ye shall kill and crucify, and some of them shall ye scourge in your synagogues, and persecute them from city to city; that upon you may come all the righteous blood shed upon the earth, from the blood of righteous Abel unto the blood of *Zacharias, son of Barachias*, whom ye slew between the Temple and the altar. Verily I say unto you, all these things shall come upon this generation."

For here we see, from the language of Jesus himself, that it was not he who was slain by Pontius Pilate, since this Zacharias, the son of Barachias, was killed in the Temple during the siege of Jerusalem, over thirty years after Pilate's recall. The event is recorded by Josephus. No *other Zacharias*, son of *Barachias*, suffered such a fate, and he was a contemporary of the historical Jesus, and not of Pontius Pilate. There was one other Zacharias, indeed, who was stoned, but he was not the son of Baruch, and he met his end, as Josephus tells us, long before Pilate's day.

That this historical Jesus of Josephus is really the personage referred to by those who write the story of the traditional Jesus, is matter, however, of no mere isolated proof. This proof abounds; it is supplied by Josephus and St. Luke, and corroborated by St. Matthew, and is not merely a myth, and it would be absurd to resolve the whole story into this;—he was a real personage, who must have left record of himself in history, and no trace of him can be found in Pontius Pilate's time. Of the prophet of that period history tells a different tale. We have shown the man whom the four Greek writers mistook for Jesus. We have shown that those great events which are related as coincident with the life of Jesus, did not take place in the time of Pilate. We have shown that they did take place at the time of the historical Jesus. We have shown that Simon Peter refers to those events as having happened within his experience, and that they are recorded as historical facts by a contemporary as having happened in the last years preceding the destruction of Jerusalem, and as having, from their portentous character, astonished the Judean and the Roman worlds. Enough all this to account for the miraculous element that suffuses the traditional accounts.

With such demonstrative evidence in proof, is it audacious in us to throw down this challenge to the world and defy it to controvert the facts adduced?

The reference of the history in debate to the days of Pontius Pilate is without a single support in fact; indeed, it is unconsciously refuted by the chronology of St. Luke. The four Greek writers could but rely upon traditional information alone for their chronology, and as there was evidence which had reached Rome that a pretender to divine inspiration had been executed by Pontius Pilate, it was accepted by them as the period of the events which they relate. It was adopted when all the living witnesses who could have corrected them were dead, and on the best evidence they had; for it must be remembered that the person in question is represented to have been a great deluder of the people, to have led captive many who clung to him and shared his fate. Nevertheless there is abundant evidence to satisfy the candid lover of truth that not a word of Jesus can be traced to the period referred to. The religion of Jesus, so far from existing in Pontius Pilate's time, is undiscoverable up to the date of the fall of Jerusalem; and no other religion is traceable to that age, except that of Judas of Galilee, which had already seen the light by the time when, according to Luke, Jesus was born. As presumptive evidence that Jesus has in tradition been confounded with this Judas, we have already referred to the fact that in the traditional accounts James, who is called the brother of the Lord, is also called the brother of Judas.

But be this as it may; what we have advanced rests upon no uncertain data; novel though it be, it has a foundation that cannot be shaken; it is not put forth as a theory, but as a fact—a fact hitherto unrecognised and unthought of, because the chronology proved so misleading. This one speck of error, enlarging till it filled the entire field of vision, has availed to hide the facts of the case and balk all attempts at rational explanation. The one black spot which has developed into a darkness that has obscured the whole subject, is the unhistorical reference of the character and actions of one individual to another without a name, who lived and died thirty years earlier.

The coincidences, however, are such, so characteristic and so numerous, between the accounts of Josephus and the Gospels as to point irrefragably to the conclusion that the traditional writers really and truly refer to the historical Jesus, and not to any one of the period of Pontius Pilate, when no wonderful incidents took place, and when it would be impossible to have concealed them, had they done so. The historical Jesus can be otherwise identified as the personage whom the traditional writers refer to. Do they not say that he was possessed by a divine passion? Do they not say that he preached, denouncing evil to the nation, in the Temple, the synagogues, and in the byeways? Do they not say that he was fed by the people, giving no thanks? Do they not say that he prophesied the destruction of the Temple, and used the same expressions of woe? Do they not say that he was brought before the Sanhedrim and scourged and scorned? Do they not say that he was brought before the procurator, and underwent torture, till his very bones were laid bare? Do they not say that he refused to beg for mercy, and to open his lips in judgment against those who then ill-used him? Do they not say that he was regarded by his brethren as beside himself? Do they not say his name was Jesus, and that he foretold his decease at Jerusalem? Do they not speak of great miracles and prodigies having then taken place, such as the light over the prison of Peter during the night, and the great gate opening of itself at that very Passover, and the wonders at Pentecost, with its strange sounds and shaking of the place? Do they not say that Jesus cursed the generation that killed Zacharias, the son of Barachias, who was slain in the Temple? Do they not mix up what belongs to this meek Jesus with what belongs to the other fierce Galilean Jesus, his contemporary? Do they not represent his followers as poor Galilean fishermen? Do they not mention the names of Simon and John? Do they not report that Simon was thrown into prison and miraculously released? Do they not say that Jesus was a great innovator, but a great upholder of the law and commandments of Moses? Do they not picture him as a man of violence, who advised his band of followers to sell their belongings and buy a sword? Do they not say he was betrayed by one of his followers immediately after this event?

Coincidences such as these are chronicled by Josephus as historical events which happened in his own time. He could not be mistaken, as the Evangelists were, who went by traditions in the lips of grandchildren; and there is both internal and external evidence to vouch for his fidelity. Can we say as much for the traditional writers? What further proof need we give of their untrustworthy character?

CHAPTER XVII.

The fall of the Holy City due to the expectation of a Messiah—Supposed sign of a new economy—Christianity dates from the memory of him who predicted its downfall—The mention of the Jesus of the Gospels in Josephus a forgery—Date of Paul's Epistles.

THE fall of Jerusalem and the destruction of the holy Temple by Titus had an almost incredible influence upon the political and religious institutions of the world. The affection of the Jewish race for their holy city and its Temple, justly reckoned the wonder of the world, knew no bounds. Nor was this veneration confined to them; the holy place was regarded with more or less of awe by all who had seen it, or heard of it by report; and it was something more than a tradition, it was a religious belief, that the Creator of the world was its architect. Its construction at the command of the Most High, the tradition of its original splendour, its association with the religious life and literature of so singular a people, and the sublime purity of its ritual, all conspired to invest it with sentiments of sacredness, felt towards no other temple upon earth. Titus, baffled by the strategy and courage of the besieged, with fiery resentment raging at his heart, paused to consider how, in punishing the city, he might save the Temple from destruction, lest horror at the act should bring execration upon himself. He sent Josephus again and again to his countrymen to persuade them to relent, and protested that the responsibility would be theirs, and not his, if their obstinacy should compel him to doom their city and its Temple to a common fate. Posterity should bear in mind, and particularly Jewish posterity, that not by his hand, but by their own ancestors, the ruin was wrought; for Titus offered them the olive branch before it was too late, and they waived it off.

What, then, it may be asked, drove the infatuated people to maintain such a desperate resistance in the face of famine, fire, and sword, pestilence within, and overwhelming odds without? Was it the idea of a new Jerusalem? Not the shadow of such an idea had as yet occurred to the most fanatical head. Was it the advent of the new dispensation? Neither had Bedlam published any tidings of this. Was it the new religion of Jesus of Galilee? There was no new religion of Jesus of Galilee, only that of one Judas of Galilee. Had the mad fanaticism its origin in the sect that sprang up phoenix-like out of the ashes of the Pontius Pilate pretender? Both he and his followers along with him had passed away thirty years before, and the memory of them was forgotten in the troubles that had come. What, then, was it which brought on the people such dire infatuation? Let the truthful historian of the period answer?

"Now, if any one consider these things, he will find that God takes care of mankind, and by all means possible foreshows to our race what is for their preservation, but that men perish by those miseries which they madly and voluntarily bring upon themselves; for the Jews, by demolishing the tower of Antonia, had made their Temple four-square, while at the same time they had it written in their sacred oracles that 'then should their city be taken, as well as their holy house, when once their Temple should become four-square.' But now, what did most elevate them in undertaking this war was an ambiguous oracle, that was also found in their sacred writings, how '*about that time one from their country should become governor of the habitable earth.*' The Jews took this prediction to belong to themselves in particular, and many of the wise men were thereby deceived in their determination. Now this oracle certainly denoted the government of Vespasian, who was appointed emperor in Judea. However, it is not possible for men to avoid fate, although they see it beforehand. But these men interpreted some of these signals according to their own pleasure, and some of them they utterly despised, until their madness was demonstrated, both by the taking of their city and their own destruction."*

It was, then, the expectation of a Messiah, not the advent of one, which drove the Jewish people to such desperate courses. It was the new religion founded by Judas of Galilee which deluded the "younger sort" into the expectation of a divine deliverance, which resulted in the destruction of their nation and the dispersion of the race. There is the clearest proof

* "Book of the Wars," book vi. chap. 5. § 4.

which could be desired that no Messiah had appeared, and that the prediction, on the ground of which the expectation of his coming was based, had not been fulfilled. Josephus would never, in connection with these events, have said that the only sect which arose in his day taught the expectation of a Messiah if another existed which affirmed in the face of the world that he had come. The allegation of the existence of such a sect is demonstrably false, as the historian would never have denied the fact with communities all round who could have contradicted him to his face.

When the city and Temple had been destroyed, and the nation lay hopelessly prostrate under a foreign yoke, men began to reflect on the crisis that had come, and to cast about for an explanation. It was clear, it seemed, that God, in not avenging their cause, had forsaken the people He had chosen; the sacred symbols of His presence amongst them He had suffered to be trampled in the dust; they who, in their pride of privilege, had spurned other people, were become "a scorn and astonishment to all mankind;" and the "woe! woe! from the four winds" of the Jerusalem martyr sighed moaningly through the desolation of many a heart. Brooding over these sad events, men bethought themselves of a reason for the mysterious dispensation, and the theory suggested itself that the Jewish economy was of temporary duration, and that the term of its existence had now come. It confirmed this hypothesis that biblical prophecy predicted a dispersion of the people and a restoration of the city, which last began to be looked forward to as a New Jerusalem from above.

No wonder so many in the nation began to reflect on him who had predicted these dire judgments. It was by the teaching of prophets their forefathers had been guided, and the oracles these had uttered constituted the staple of their sacred books. Not that they had not reason to distrust many who claimed their regard as prophets of the Lord, but in this one the signs were unmistakable, and every syllable he uttered had been literally and fearfully fulfilled. He had gone forth, as the old prophets were wont, lifting up his voice aloud in all thoroughfares and sacred assemblies, and had reason to complain, as the rest of them had, that no one would believe his report, and sealed his commission before the rulers of the nation in martyrdom and death. All were witnesses to the truth of his denunciations, and Josephus reproaches his countrymen for disregarding his warning voice, appealing, as he does so, to the burning inspiration of his words. And not only had the Jewish people occasion to remember the apparition of this prophet; the Roman soldiers could report how the God of the Jews had sent a messenger to warn them of their rebellion, and how He, because they had recked not His servant's denunciations, had left them in their obstinacy to their fate.

If there had existed a Jesus before this one, who predicted he would reappear in that generation, as was subsequently recorded by the four Greek writers, he would have been hailed as come back in that very person himself. His history displays the same features of character, his predictions were the same, and uttered nearly in the same words, and he underwent a repetition of the same fate. If there had been any who believed in the first, they would have looked out for his reappearance in a time of the second, for the promised hour had come. It is clear, therefore, again, that the allegation of an earlier Jesus is a sheer anachronism, and that up to this time a body of Christian disciples did not exist. If any sectarian body existed then in the Jewish state, it must have been of the religion of Judas of Galilee, who, by preaching a "kingdom of God" in opposition to the Roman rule, wrought the ruin of the Jewish state. Josephus expressly mentions this sect as a pestilent one to the community, and as expressly ignores the existence of any other. It is impossible to believe that he could have thus virtually denied the Christian religion, had there existed at the time a Church professing it, with its four Gospels written in Greek, in flat affirmation of the contrary fact. Wherefore, we repeat again, if Josephus wrote untruthfully, were not his allegations questioned? Why were those Greek writings, written, as was alleged, by eye-witnesses of the character and life of Jesus, not produced, and an exposure made of the historian's unfairness and want of truth? Why, if the authors existed at the time, were they silent? If it be urged that Josephus was silent in regard to this religion and its founder on account of his prejudice against them, is it to be thought that the public preachers of Christianity remained silent from kindred feelings? Was it because they were alarmed for their own safety that they said nothing, when they dared to preach openly in defiance of both the Roman authority and Jewish Sanhedrim that Jesus was Christ? Did they not meet together and band themselves into a brotherhood to promulgate the truth of the very divinity of this Messiah? Wherefore was this in an age full of enthusiasm? How did it happen that an age so much on the alert for signs and wonders should take no note of these, and the writings which graphically foretold the judgment that had overtaken it? The answer to this is that these writings did not exist; they could not be known to posterity, and escape the knowledge of contemporaries. The writings of the Elder Pliny, of Seneca, of Justus, and of Josephus, were known to their contemporaries, as those of Cicero, of Philo, of Demosthenes, and a thousand others, were known to theirs; but the history of the most wonderful character that had ever appeared and the most wonderful events that had ever occurred in the world, although committed to writing, was not only not known at the time, but the facts of it were denied years after by the historian of the period, in a narrative in which he details all that had been publicly said and done in Judea from before the procuratorship of Pilate to nearly sixty years after.

It would almost seem as if the historians of the

period, writing freely on the opinions of all sects and the public transactions of all nations, had entered into a conspiracy to withhold from the knowledge of the world the story of those events, and as if the four Greek writers, if they were of the period of Pontius Pilate, as well as Paul, had been parties to the conspiracy, and the documents they withheld had been smuggled and published in the second century. They must have consented too, to concealing their own writings during their own lifetime, and the epistles, if they were written at the time specified, must have been marked PRIVATE AND CONFIDENTIAL, considering the lapse of time that passed before their contents were known to the world; and these epistles had not only been written, but read to congregations of the period, referring to a gospel and doctrine that had been preached far and wide, and formed matter of public notoriety from end to end of the Judean, and large sections even of the Gentile world. The doctrine these epistles represent as preached everywhere was that the Son of God had come in the flesh and given power to man on earth to do what would be ratified in heaven. This doctrine had been proclaimed, as it were, on the very housetops, and the community far and near had received the glad tidings with joy as more than a pledge of eternal salvation.

If Paul, as is alleged, wrote in the days of Claudius Cæsar and Nero, his writings must have been extant during the early life and manhood of Josephus, and yet this historian denies the existence, root and branch, of the Christian religion and its founder, and repeats that denial in the fifty-sixth year of his life as follows :—

"And now it will not be perhaps an invidious thing, if I treat briefly of my own family, and of the actions of my own life, while there are still living such as can either prove what I say to be false, or can attest that it is true; with which account I shall put an end to these Antiquities, which are contained in twenty books, and sixty thousand verses. And if God permit me, I will briefly run over this war again, with what befell us therein to this very day, which is the thirteenth year of the reign of Cæsar Domitian, and the fifty-sixth year of my own life." *

Here we have Josephus, half a century after the recall of Pontius Pilate, challenging his contemporaries to deny anything he had written up to that period, and among the statements challenged are those which affirm that no other sect had arisen in his day except that of Judas of Galilee, no other ascetic corresponding to John the Baptist except Banus, and no other Jesus of a public character except the meek one of Jerusalem and the violent Galilean, of whom and their activities he first and he last gives any historical notice. Nowhere in all his writings is there mention of Jesus Christ or his sect, except one clumsily and barefacedly inserted in his pages after his decease by a daring interpolator. The mention we

* "Antiquities," book xx. chap. 11, § 2.

refer to is made in the "Antiquities of the Jews," book xviii. cap. 3, § 3, and occurs in the following terms :—

"Now there was about this time Jesus, a wise man, if it be lawful to call him a man, for he was a doer of wonderful works, a teacher of such men as receive the truth with pleasure. He drew over to him both many of the Jews and many of the Gentiles. He was (the) Christ. And when Pilate, at the suggestion of the principal men among us, had condemned him to the cross, those that loved him at the first did not forsake him; for he appeared to them alive again the third day; as the divine prophets had foretold these and ten thousand other wonderful things concerning him. And the tribe of Christians, so named from him, are not extinct at this day."

The grounds on which the genuineness of this passage is contested are many, but we must, out of respect for our readers, content ourselves with stating only a few, premising that its spuriousness, though not universally conceded, is admitted by critics of all shades of opinion.

The *first* objection to the genuineness of the paragraph is that it is a gratuitous interruption of the stream of the narrative, and has no connection with the paragraphs which precede and follow.

The *second* objection is that it is out of place, and not in the historian's manner, to make mention of the Christian tribe as "not extinct to *this day*" in a paragraph referring to the *time* of Pilate's procuratorship, *when*, as the Evangelists show, the name and sect did not exist.

The *third* objection is that in no case could Christians be called a *tribe* by Josephus, but a *sect*. That would certainly not be a proper designation for a sect of philosophy, and one, as even the four Greek writers allow, first established only long afterwards.

The *fourth* objection to this paragraph being genuine is that Josephus was committed, as the professed historian of the period, to refer to at least *some* of the "ten thousand wonderful things concerning him," had they had any reality.

The *fifth* objection lies in the fact that in that passage of his history in which he gives an account of the pretender of the Pilate period he says nothing of this far more remarkable figure, who, it is alleged, suffered under the same administration a kindred fate.

The *sixth* objection we make to the genuineness of the paragraph in question is that Josephus, in describing the new religion of Judas of Galilee, expressly asserts that no other arose in that time.

The *seventh* objection we have to offer to this impious fraud is that when Josephus accounts for the obstinacy of the Jews at the siege of Jerusalem by reference to a widespread expectation that a Messiah *was coming*, he says nothing at all *then* of a Messiah *having come* and risen from the dead, "as the divine prophets had foretold." That expectation was simply represented as arising from an ambiguous oracle that was found in their sacred writings, how about this time one from their country should become governor of the habitable earth.

Now the perpetrators of this forgery, or pious fraud, as it is more mildly called, must have seen the necessity of some confirmation from the pen of the historian of the period of the wonderful events which the later Greek writers averred had taken place in those preceding years; but in their haste to commit the fraud,—which, by the by, is not in every copy of Josephus,—they did not reflect upon the fact that Josephus had already and elsewhere referred to an insignificant prophet of the date, and never mentioned the name of Jesus of Nazareth. They did not reflect that he had already named all the sects that had appeared in Judea fifty-six years after Pilate's recall, and had nowhere spoken of the sect of the Christians, but by implication asserted their non-existence. They did not reflect that his testimony in regard to the non-existence of Christianity was confirmed by another historian of the period, Justus, whose only quarrel with Josephus respected not a historical but a political question, and hinged on the charges each brought against the other of having accelerated the ruin of the country. They did not reflect that Josephus had furnished an account of another Jesus, who was instinct with the same spirit, had uttered the same woes, and suffered the same fate, amid similar miraculous attendant circumstances. They did not reflect that the historian, whom in their interpolation they make skip over all the ten thousand wonderful prophetic fulfilments in the career of the traditional Jesus, is the very man who historically relates all these so-called wonderful fulfilments and refers them to the proper period of their occurrence, towards the fall of Jerusalem And finally, these interpolators were not aware that St. Luke, by unconsciously referring the time of the birth of Jesus to the period of the Cyrenian taxation, oversets the reckoning which fixes the death of Jesus at the period of the Pilate procuratorship. But the pious fraud practised by these forgers, history tells us, was part of a system which had the sanction of the early Church. The pages of Gibbon [*] will supply evidence in confirmation :—

"The 'Apology' of Tertullian," he says, "contains two very ancient, very singular, but at the same time very suspicious, instances of imperial clemency; the edicts published by Tiberius and by Marcus Antoninus, and designed not only to protect the innocence of the Christians, but even to proclaim those stupendous miracles which had attested the truth of their doctrine. The first of these examples is attended with some difficulties which might perplex the sceptical mind. We are required to believe that Pontius Pilate informed the Emperor of the unjust sentence of death which he had pronounced against an innocent, and, as it appeared, a divine person, and that without acquiring the merit he exposed himself to the danger of martyrdom; that Tiberius, who avowed his contempt for all religion, immediately conceived the design of placing the Jewish Messiah among the gods of Rome; that his servile senate ventured to disobey the commands of their master; that Tiberius, instead of resenting their refusal, contented himself

---

[*] "Decline and Fall of the Roman Empire," chap. vi. p. 409.

with protecting the Christians from the severity of the laws, *many years before such laws were enacted*, or before *the Church had assumed any distinct name or existence;* and, lastly, that the memory of this *extraordinary transaction* was preserved in the most *public* and *authentic* records, which escaped the knowledge of the historians of Greece and Rome, and were only visible to the eyes of an African Christian, who composed his 'Apology' *one hundred and sixty years after the death of Tiberius*. The edict of Marcus Antoninus is supposed to have been the effect of his devotion and gratitude for the miraculous deliverance which he had obtained in the Marcomannic war. The distress of the legions, the seasonable tempest of rain and hail, of thunder and lightning, and the dismay and defeat of the barbarians, have been celebrated by the eloquence of several pagan writers. If there were any Christians in that army, it was natural that they should ascribe some merit to the fervent prayers which in the moment of danger they had offered up for their own and the public safety. But we are still assured by monuments of brass and marble, by the imperial medals, and by the Antonine column, that neither the prince nor the people entertained any sense of this signal obligation, since they unanimously attribute their deliverance to the providence of Jupiter and to the interposition of Mercury. During the whole course of his reign, Marcus despised the Christians as a philosopher and punished them as a sovereign."

From this it will be seen that these pious frauds were perpetrated as early as a hundred and sixty years after Pontius Pilate's recall, who, if he underwent a trial at all, must have done so before the tribune of Caius Caligula, Tiberius' successor. When the Christian religion was fairly before the world, and the report of the four Greek writers respecting its origin challenged general regard, the necessity of affording some contemporary confirmation must have been felt, and the story of these two palpable frauds concedes a glimpse into the underhand manœuvring which would without scruple be resorted to to supply the desideratum. That mankind have in this matter been imposed upon is beyond all doubt, and it is for the historical student to inquire when and how the Pontius Pilate chronology was foisted upon the world by the Church. The chief drawback is, that to the great mass of the people questions of this nature are not deemed of any particular account, as they will not be persuaded that the main point is grounded in deception. Nevertheless the student of history should not abate his efforts, as thereby only can a breach be made in the Christian defences, and a passage forced into the heart of the citadel.

Many of our readers may have remarked that while we have argued for the late origin of the Gospels, we have said nothing bearing upon the date of the epistles of Paul, and it is incumbent upon us to show that they were written after the fall of Jerusalem. In proof of which position we will commence with quoting from Paul's alleged writings (1 Thess. ii. 14-16) :—

"For ye, brethren, became followers of the churches of God, which in Judea are in Christ Jesus; for ye also have suffered *like things of your own countrymen,* even as they have of the Jews, who both killed the Lord Jesus, and their own prophets, and have persecuted us; and they please not God, and are contrary to all men : forbidding us to speak to the Gentiles, that they might be saved, to fill up their sins alway; *for the wrath is come upon them to the uttermost.*"

Paul evidently alludes here to the destruction of Jerusalem and the sufferings of the Jewish people. The wrath cannot be said to have come upon them to the uttermost until the destruction of Jerusalem and the holy Temple. See again in the epistle to the Hebrews, chap. xii. 24–28 :—

"And to Jesus, the mediator of the new covenant, and to the blood of sprinkling, that speaketh better things than that of Abel. See that ye refuse not him that speaketh; *For if they escaped not who refused him that spake on earth*, much more shall not we escape, if we turn away from him that speaketh from heaven : whose voice then shook the earth : but now he hath promised, saying, Yet once more I shake not the *earth only*, but also heaven. And this word, 'Yet once more,' signifieth the removing of those things that are shaken, as of things that are made, that those things which *cannot be shaken may remain. Wherefore we receiving a kingdom which cannot be moved*, let us have grace whereby we may serve God acceptably with reverence and godly fear."

Again in Hebrews xiii. 12–14 :—

"Wherefore Jesus also, that he might sanctify the people with his own blood, suffered without the gate. Let us go forth, therefore, unto him without the camp, bearing his reproach. For here have we no continuing city, but we seek one to come."

No one can fairly come to any other conclusion than that this epistle, too, was written after the destruction of Jerusalem. It is to the Hebrews Paul is here addressing himself, and not to the Gentiles; and this language could not be used by him if the Temple and the holy city of Jerusalem had been still in existence. Notwithstanding the numerous attempts to falsify it, history proves this fact beyond all doubt, that Christianity had no existence prior to the reign of Domitian, nor was it until long after this reign that it made any progress in the world. And one of these epistles, ascribed to Paul, bears evidence of having been written when there were Christians in Cæsar's household.

In Phil. iv. 2 he writes as follows:—

"I beseech Euodias, and beseech Syntyche, that they be of the same mind in the Lord. And I entreat thee also, true yoke-fellow, help those women which laboured with me in the gospel, with *Clement also*, and with other my fellow-labourers, whose names are in the book of life. . . . Salute every saint in Christ Jesus. The brethren which are with me greet you. All the saints salute you, *chiefly they that are of Cæsar's household.*"

Nero was the Cæsar immediately prior to the fall of Jerusalem, and surely no one will be so foolish as to persuade us that there could be saints in the household of Nero, of Vespasian, or of Domitian. History, too, points to a much later period, when Cæsar's household consisted chiefly of the saints known to Paul; and as the declaration is made by Paul himself, it is surely not too much to expect that our version of the chronology should be regarded as fully borne out by an array of proofs all conducting to the conclusion that the new dispensation was conceived after the fall of Jerusalem.

CHAPTER XVIII.

A coincidence of note—The Messianic enthusiasm from Galilee—Blending of characters, and confusion of dates—The anointing of Jesus—John's Revelations—Failure of the attempt to deify man—Conclusion.

AFTER the destruction of Jerusalem much respect was shown to Josephus by Titus, who both listened to his counsels and acceded to his requests. And this is what Josephus relates in his Life, chap. 67:—

"When I was sent by Titus Cæsar with Cerealius and a thousand horsemen to a certain village called Thecoa, in order to know whether it were a place fit for a camp, as I came back, I saw many captives crucified, and remembered three of them as my *former acquaintance*. I was very sorry at this in my mind, and went with tears in my eyes to Titus, and told him of them; so he immediately commanded them to be taken down and to have the greatest care taken of them, in order to their recovery; yet two of them died under the physician's hands, while the *third recovered*."

Now we do not say that this is the original of the following from Luke, but certainly the coincidences are very remarkable. There is a Joseph, a counsellor, a rich man and a just, in both, with three men under crucifixion, of whom two die, and one is as good as restored to life again (Luke xxiii. 49-52):

"And all his *acquaintance*, and the women that followed him from Galilee, stood afar off beholding these things. And behold there was a man named *Joseph*, a counsellor, and he was a good man, and a just. *The same had not consented to the counsel and deed of them.* He was of Arimathea, a city of the Jews, who also himself waited for the kingdom of God. This man went unto Pilate, and begged the body of Jesus."

These may be only coincidences, and we do not attach much importance to the circumstance, but it does seem strange that no other person referred to by the four Greek writers is designated, as here, by the name of a "*counsellor*," and that this should be the position of Josephus towards the Roman authorities, while the description of the traditional writer, "a good man and a just," with equal truth applies to him; neither had he "consented to the counsel and deed of them," so far, at any rate, as concerned the continuance of the war.

Certain it is, however, that many sections of the traditional story are mere combinations of events drawn from the pages of the Bible and Josephus, just as many of its doctrines are from pre-existent philosophies. We have already referred, in the latter regard, to the incarnate deity Krishna, "the saviour of men," and we may add, that very likely the story of this personage suggested to Christendom the idea of one who was slain from the foundation of the world.

Certainly the doctrine cannot mean that the Eternal was slain and then ceased to be; this application of it would entirely upset Christianity; and it is well to have an equivocation like this to fall back upon, even though recourse to it may do away with the idea of the deity of Jesus. We do not intend, however, to attach any weight to these theories, however reasonable they may appear, because of the difficulty of ever arriving at a certain result; and it would be unwise on our part to commit ourselves to any hypothesis of a questionable nature when we have solid historical data to rely upon to establish our main thesis, that the meek Jesus, the *prophet* of *Jerusalem*, is beyond all doubt the traditional Jesus of the four Gospels. The writers of these, along with Paul, themselves support by their unconscious testimony this very conclusion, opposed though it is to the express aim of their writings.

Their express assertion is in conflict with Plutarch, Seneca, the elder Pliny, Josephus, and Justus, all of whom were either actual contemporaries of Pontius Pilate or at least contemporaries of those who were. If Josephus did not himself see the light that appeared in the Pontius Pilate period, he saw and conversed at any rate with living witnesses of the events of his procuratorship, with whom may be numbered his parents and elder brother. He had to make the most minute inquiries concerning the procurator and his government of Judea, for he is the first historian who had to deal with this period, as he does in his

Antiquities, and his Wars of the Jews. It is he who furnishes the account, as we have had occasion repeatedly to remark, of the deluder of the people, killed by order of that governor; and the period of his death corresponds with that of the death of the traditional Jesus. The period of signs and wonders, too, handed down by unquestioned and undoubted history, is the period of the historical Jesus (who is himself one of the wonders), and not the period of Pontius Pilate. These signs and wonders, partly in the heavens and partly earthly signs, were known and related as matters of notoriety by the living historian of the period, who published his writings, too, while the witnesses of those things were still alive to testify to the truthfulness of his narrative.

The Pontius Pilate deluder of the people never pretended to be the Messiah, who was not expected at that period; nor was there any new religion then except the religion of Judas of Galilee. Heaven and earth combined to establish the fact, by signs and wonders from above and from below, that the so-called Messianic period is literally the period of the historical Jesus. St. Luke shows by his reference of his birth to the date of the Cyrenian taxation that the traditional Jesus was only a stripling at the recall of Pilate, and the writings of the other three Greek writers, as well as those of Paul, oblige us to assign a more modern date to the events they relate than they themselves do. Paul's allusion to the punishment "to the uttermost" which came upon the

Jews, and to their having no continuing city, points evidently to the destruction of the city as an accomplished fact; while his reference "to the saints chiefly of Cæsar's household," conduct inevitably to the conclusion that he wrote long after the fall of Jerusalem; and indeed it was during the siege of that doomed city that the historical Jesus came by his death, which he himself had predicted. The historical critic should have known that there could be no saints in Cæsar's household until after Domitian, who was the third Cæsar from his father Vespasian, and in whose reign Jerusalem succumbed;—how long after precisely we leave it to others to say, as the general chronology for which we argue is conceded by the acceptance of the historical truth, which proves that he wrote long after the fall of Jerusalem.

It is not at all improbable that some of the peculiarities of the Pontius Pilate pretender may have been blended with those of the subsequent Jesus, the more especially as we have such evidence already of a *penchant* on the part of the Greek writers for such combinations. We have in previous chapters shown how these writers have attempted to blend into one the character and creed of the Galilean with those of the meek Jesus, and we have adduced evidence to establish the conclusion arrived at by us, that the generous and meek spirit of the historical Jesus had the effect of darkening the perception of qualities which, had they been nakedly exhibited or otherwise combined, would have been pronounced unworthy the character of an ordinarily good man. Jesus of Galilee was essentially an innovator and a follower of Judas of Galilee, the founder of a sect whose shibboleth was the kingdom of God in a political sense, as implying liberty simply in the sense of immunity from a foreign yoke. The laws of God that sect affected to make their only rule and the Most High their only king, while respect to a foreign governor they regarded as idolatry and hateful to God. This sentiment would not have been so pernicious to public virtue if it had only been at all practicable; but the Roman domination was universal, and no earthly power was strong enough to resist its yoke. The Jewish nation, however, was divided between superstition and common sense, while civil strife added both to its weakness and its guilt, inducing a chronic disorder that was incurable. Those who looked to the interposition of the Messiah deluded themselves and their followers, and became the inveterate enemies of their peaceable countrymen who disagreed with their philosophy.

The Messianic enthusiasm hailed chiefly from Galilee, and was the source of great crimes and much evil to the state. A passage from Gibbon* will at this stage be appropriate :—

"At the distance of sixty years, it was the duty of the annalist to adopt the narratives of contemporaries; but it was natural for the philosopher to indulge himself in a description of the origin, the progress, and the character of the new sect, not so

---

* Gibbon's "Decline and Fall of the Roman Empire," vol. i. chap. 16.

much according to the knowledge or the prejudices of the age of Nero, as according to those of the time of Hadrian. Tacitus very frequently trusts to the curiosity or reflection of his readers to supply those intermediate circumstances and ideas which, in his extreme conciseness, he has thought proper to suppress. We may, therefore, presume to imagine some probable cause which could direct the cruelty of Nero against the Christians of Rome, whose obscurity as well as innocence should have shielded them from his indignation, and even from his notice. The Jews, who were numerous in the capital, and oppressed in their own country, were a much fitter object for the suspicions of the Emperor and of the people; nor did it seem unlikely that a vanquished nation, who already discovered their abhorrence of the Roman yoke, might have recourse to the most atrocious means of gratifying their implacable revenge. But the Jews possessed very powerful advocates in the palace, and even in the heart of the tyrant, his wife and mistress, the beautiful Poppæa, and a favourite player of the race of Abraham, who had already employed their intercession in behalf of the obnoxious people. In their room it was necessary to offer some other victims, and it might easily be suggested that, although the genuine followers of Moses were innocent of the fire of Rome, there had arisen among them a new and *pernicious sect of Galileans, which was capable of the most horrid crimes. Under the appellation of Galileans two distinctions of men were confounded, the most opposite to each other in their manner and principles*—the disciples who had embraced the faith of Jesus of Nazareth, and the zealots who had followed the standard of Judas the Gaulonite. The *former were the friends, the latter were the enemies of human kind*, and the only resemblance between them consisted in the same inflexible constancy, which in the defence of their cause *rendered them insensible of death and tortures.*"

This testimony, confirmed by that of the learned Dr. Lardner,* is of great weight, justifying, as it does, the condemnatory judgment we have pronounced on the Galilean Jesus and his associates, whose character and principles were so diametrically opposed to those of the meek Jesus and his followers. The former were the enemies of mankind, and the latter were the friends, and the friendly and unfriendly principles of both are sought to be united into one by the four Greek writers. And the incongruity of the amalgam must be as obvious to the philosopher as to the historian. The friendship exemplified was of a beautiful type, full of self-abnegation and charity, and the meekness evinced a piety and devotion the very opposite of what proceeds from enmity.

But let the two characters once more speak for themselves (Matt. xix. 17–20) :—

"Why callest thou me *good?* There is none good but *one,* that is, God ; but if thou wilt enter into life, keep the commandments. He saith unto him, *Which?* Jesus said, Thou shalt do no murder, Thou shalt not commit adultery, Thou shalt not steal, Thou shalt not bear false witness, Honour thy father and thy mother, and, Thou shalt love thy neighbour as thyself."

Mark the difference of character implied in the following, how incompatible it is with the above (St.

---

* The learned Dr. Lardner ("Jewish and Heathen Testimonies," vol. ii. pp. 102, 103) *has proved* that the name of Galilean was a very ancient, and perhaps the primitive, appellation of the Christians.

Luke xxii. 36) : "Then said he unto them, But now, he that hath a purse, let him take it, and likewise his scrip; and he that hath no sword, let him sell his garment and buy one." And in chap. ix. 59, "And he said unto another, Follow me. But he said, Lord, suffer me first to go and bury my father. Jesus said unto him, Let the dead bury their dead, but go thou and preach the kingdom of God," *the cry of the Zealots.* Again, take John xi. 25 : " Jesus said unto her, I am the resurrection and the life ; he that believeth in me, though he were dead, yet shall he live."

Now when we compare these sentiments, we can, as we again insist, arrive at no other conclusion than that it was impossible for the same lips to utter them all. In the first set of verses, the man Jesus confesses to his own imperfection and the absolute, unapproachable goodness of God, hinges the hope of eternal life on, among other pieties, respect for father and mother, and sums up all duty and all blessedness in loving one's neighbour as one's self. In the subsequent three verses we have a violent appeal to arms, in behalf of a kingdom that he elsewhere says is to conquer by meekness, a command to dishonour a dead parent by leaving him unburied, and instead of a humble acknowledgment of his impotence, there is an assumption of power to bring the dead to life. These inconsistencies we adduce as extreme ones, arising from the blending of the two Jesuses; but the like are traceable throughout the narratives from which they come. No two classes of maxims can be more opposed to each other than those embodied in the above extracts: they cannot co-exist in the same system or bear the stamp of the same seal. Either may be taken up and taught separately, both cannot be enforced together. If the principles first quoted commend themselves to our admiration and acceptance, those which follow certainly merit our reprobation and rejection.

The majority of Christians have hitherto not dared to take exception to the actions and sentiments of the traditional Jesus, but have regarded them as divinely perfect. They first raise the man to an equality with God, and then regard what he says and does as the sayings and doings of deity. The deity is brought down in nature and sentiment to the level of man; not so easily can the human be carried up into the divine; and here accordingly the attempt ends in signal failure. It is easier to lower the sublime attributes of God to the ideas of man than to make the everyday attributes of man worthy of divinity. When a man is exalted to a superhuman level, which he not unfrequently is in the besotted regard of his fellow-mortals, his acts and utterances are apt to be regarded as above the criticism of an ordinary standard. They are estimated out of regard to the source from which they come, and not according to their intrinsic merits and demerits. If the character of the Galilean Jesus had been more objectionable than it is, it would be accepted in all probability with not less veneration. It is no doubt proper to regard whatever comes from

God as good, but what comes from man should not be received as having come from the same source. What comes from man may be criticised, and when, as in the present case, we see the blending of a loving self-sacrificing spirit with a fleshly, we are free to pronounce it as worthy or unworthy of devotion.

The generosity of Jesus is put to the test by the suggestion that the box of spikenard with which he was anointed should be disposed of for the benefit of the poor, instead of being used on his person. He justifies the action with the words, "The poor ye have always with you, but me ye have not always." But the most incredible feature in this transaction is not the indifference expressed to the wants of the poor, so much as the distinction he derives from being anointed by a repentant reprobate, bringing honour upon himself and blessing upon her. For here are two inconceivabilities: first, that God should feel honoured by the homage of such a woman, and, second, that he should exalt her above the unfallen. To have mercy on the wicked is a gracious act, but to exalt the wicked above the virtuous, while it is an incentive to the former to become good, is no less an incentive to the latter to become bad, in order to obtain the higher reward bestowed on the repentant. That Jesus should signify his appreciation of a great affection in return for a great forgiveness is intelligible, but not that he, being divine, should prefer the homage of such an one over every other.

We have already animadverted sufficiently on the

evidence furnished by Paul as to the error in the chronology which refers the life and death of Jesus to the Pontius Pilate period, and we have deduced the same conclusion from data supplied by St. Luke. We have also shown that the language of Jesus points to events which happened in the last years of Jerusalem, and that the signs and wonders witnessed by Simon belong to the same period. It now behoves us to analyse briefly the record of John, if indeed such writings can be looked upon as at all of any historical value; but as they are so often appealed to in defence of the accepted theology, we are entitled to avail ourselves of their help in fortifying our position in regard to the fallibility of these documents. This John, the divine, like the other Greek writers his colleagues, proceeds unconsciously upon the principle that cause and effect are identical, and scarcely deems it necessary to guard against this charge, which might so naturally be preferred against his reasoning. Starting from the book of Genesis (chap. i. 3,) "And God said, Let there be light, and there was light," he arrives at the idea of the *Logos* or Word: (St. John i. 1–4.) "In the beginning was the Word, and the Word was with God, and the Word was God. The same was in the beginning with God. All things were made by him, and without him was not anything made that was made. In him was life, and the life was the light of men."

It is clear, we think, that this doctrine of the Logos is derived by John from the words said to have been pronounced by God when He commanded light out of darkness; only this commandment, or *word* of God, is assumed by John to be God Himself: "In Him was life, and the life was the light of men." Now, if we are to take the words of God as God Himself, His unity will be in the same position in which it now stands, for it has been pluralised already by the doctrine of the Trinity, only this doctrine will also be subverted, if we adopt this unphilosophical idea, and take, as this author does, cause for effect, or rather effect for cause. This adaptation of St. John, which is not a revelation, so far at least as the premises are concerned, will not bear investigation; for if so subjected, the premises will be found wrongly taken, and the conclusion wrongly drawn. From the expression, "*And the Word was God*," Christianity derives the doctrine of a substantial divinity, which might be simply figurative. Why should this Word of God be deemed the deity, more than any other word of His? The answer to this query will be, that in this special case "The Word was light," and that the only-begotten Son of God is light. But such an explanation is a sophistical and unnatural one, since, as is well known to theologians, the light spoken of in Genesis is of a physical character, proceeding from a spiritual source indeed, being the work of God, but still a reflective substance, as part of the creation of the Creator, conveying the perception of visible objects to the sight, and not spiritual ones to the mind.

St. John's writings are equally delusive in many

other respects. His picture of the "New Jerusalem" is not in its details a new revelation, or more original than that of the Logos, although his deductions are entitled to some merit in point of originality. In order to justify this charge, it will be necessary to transcribe some of the particulars relating to the old Jerusalem and its Temple, as given by Josephus.*

"Now all those of the stock of the priests that could not minister by reason of some defect in their bodies came within the partition, together with those that had no such imperfection, and had their share with them by reason of their stock, but still made use of none, except their own private garments, for nobody but he that officiated had on his sacred garments; but then those priests that were without any blemish upon them went up to the altar clothed in fine linen. They abstained chiefly from wine out of this fear, lest otherwise they should transgress some rules of their ministration. The high priest did also go up with them; not always indeed, but on the seventh days and new moons, and if any festivals belonging to our nation, which we celebrate every year, happened. When he officiated, he had on a pair of breeches, that reached below his thighs, and had on an inner garment of linen, together with a blue garment round, without seam, with fringe-work and reaching to the feet. There were also golden bells, that hung upon the fringes, and pomegranates intermixed among them. The bells signified thunder and the pomegranates lightning. But that girdle that tied the garment to the breast was embroidered with five rows of various colours, of gold, and purple, and scarlet, as also of fine linen and blue, with which

---

* "Wars of the Jews," Book v. chap. 5, §§ 7, 8.

colours we told you before the veils of the Temple were embroidered also. The like embroidery was upon the ephod, but the quantity of gold thereon was greater. Its figure was that of a stomacher for the breast. There were upon it two golden buttons like small shields, which buttoned the ephod to the garment; in these buttons were enclosed two large and very excellent sardonyxes, *having the names of the tribes of that nation* engraved upon them: on the other part there hung *twelve stones, three in a row one way and four in the other*; *a sardius, a topaz,* and an *emerald, a carbuncle, a jasper,* and a *sapphire,* an *agate,* an *amethyst,* and a *ligure,* an *onyx, a beryl,* and a *chrysolite, upon every one of which was again engraved one of the fore-mentioned names of the tribes.* A mitre also of fine linen encompassed his head, which was tied by a blue riband, about which there was another golden crown, in which was engraven the sacred name (of God); it consists of four vowels. However, the high priest did not wear these garments at other times, but a more plain habit; he only did it when he went into the most sacred part of the Temple, which he did but once a year, on that day when our custom is for all of us to keep a fast to God. And thus much concerning the city and the Temple, but for the customs and laws hereto relating, we shall speak more accurately another time, for there remain a great many things thereto relating which have not been here touched upon.

"Now as to the tower of Antonia, it was situated at the corner of two cloisters of the court of the Temple, of that on the west and that on the north; it was erected upon a rock of fifty cubits in height, and was on a great precipice; it was the work of King Herod, wherein he demonstrated his natural magnanimity. In the first place, the rock itself was covered over with *smooth pieces of stone from its foundation,* both

for ornament, and that any one who would either try
to get up or to go down it might not be able to hold
his feet upon it. Next to this, and before you come
to the edifice of the tower itself, *there was a wall
three cubits high,* but within *that wall all the space of
the tower of Antonia itself was built upon to the height
of forty cubits.* The inward parts had the largeness
and form of a palace, it being parted into all kinds of
rooms and other conveniences, such as courts, and
places for bathing, and broad spaces for camps; insomuch that, by having all conveniences that cities
wanted, it might seem to be composed of several
cities; but by its magnificence it seemed a palace;
and as the entire structure resembled that of a tower,
it contained also four other distinct towers at its four
corners, whereof the others were but fifty cubits high,
whereas that which lay upon the south-east corner
was seventy cubits high, that from thence the whole
Temple might be viewed; but on the corner where
it joined to the two cloisters of the Temple, it had
passages down to them both, through which the
guards (for there always lay in this tower a Roman
legion) went several ways among the cloisters with
their arms on the Jewish festivals, in order to watch
the people, that they might not then attempt to
make any innovations; for the Temple was a fortress
that guarded the city, as was the tower of Antonia
a guard to the Temple; and in that tower were the
guards of those three. There was also a peculiar
fortress belonging to the upper city, which was
Herod's palace; but for the hill Bezetha, it was divided
from the tower of Antonia, as we have already told
you; and as that hill on which the tower of Antonia
stood was the highest of these three, so did it adjoin
to the new city, and was the only place that hindered
the sight of the Temple on the north. And this shall
suffice at present to have spoken about the city and

the walls about it, because I have proposed to myself to make a more accurate description of it elsewhere."

It is not necessary for our purpose to transcribe more from this elaborate description, as we have given enough to establish the general resemblance between it and the sketch given by St. John of the New Jerusalem, and to prove to our readers that St. John, or at least the person who assumed his name, had, if he did not copy from Josephus, painted the picture which he gives, not as seen in a heavenly vision, but after the plan and in the terms of a terrestrial structure. Here is his description (Rev. xxi. 9–23) :—

"And there came unto me one of the seven angels, which had the seven vials full of the seven last plagues, and talked with me, saying, Come hither, I will show thee the bride, the Lamb's wife. And he carried me away in the spirit to a great and high mountain, and showed me that great city, the holy Jerusalem, descending out of heaven from God, having the glory of God; and her light was like unto a stone most precious, even like a jasper stone, clear as crystal, and had a wall great and high, and had twelve gates, and at the gates twelve angels, and names written thereon, which are the names of the twelve tribes of the children of Israel. On the east three gates, on the north three gates, on the south three gates, and on the west three gates. And the wall of the city had twelve foundations, and in them the names of the twelve Apostles of the Lamb. And he that talked with me had a golden reed to measure the city, and the gates thereof, and the wall thereof. And the city lieth four-square, and the length is as large as the breadth; and he measured the city with the reed, twelve thousand furlongs. The length and the breadth and the height of it are equal. And he measured the wall thereof, an hundred and forty and four cubits, according to the measure of a man, that is, of the angel. And the building of the wall of it was of jasper, and the city was pure gold like unto clear glass. And the foundations of the wall of the city were garnished with all manner of precious stones. The first foundation was jasper, the second sapphire, the third a chalcedony, the fourth an emerald, the fifth sardonyx, the sixth sardius, the seventh chrysolite, the eighth beryl, the ninth a topaz, the tenth a chrysoprasus, the eleventh a jacinth, the twelfth an amethyst. And the twelve gates were twelve pearls; every several gate was of one pearl; and the street of the city was pure gold, as it were transparent glass. And I saw no temple therein, for the Lord God Almighty and the Lamb are the temple of it. And the city had no need of the sun, neither of the moon, to shine in it, for the glory of God did lighten it, and the Lamb is the light thereof."

This will suffice to establish the probability that the writer of the Revelation, in penning this description, had before him a copy of Josephus, who in another place refers to the Temple as being four-square, and who in divers portions of his work supplies much information respecting the New Jerusalem by simple descriptions of the old, just as, strange to say, St. John supplies much information respecting the old Jerusalem by simple descriptions of the New. Indeed, the latter appears to be throughout indebted to the Bible and to the works of Josephus at once for his imagery and his philosophy, resolving on the one hand the biblical doctrine of the word of God into the second person of the Trinity, and transferring the historical description of the old Jerusalem, with a few extra gems of gigantic size and brilliancy, into his picture of the new. And indeed this spiritual Jerusalem is of the earth earthy ; precious metals are in great abundance in a place where they are supposed to be of no account; streets of gold, and pearly gates, and a huge array of vulgar glitter and barbaric grandeur. But while we are obliged to St. John for this gorgeous description of the heavenly city and the graphic account he gives of the mysterious drama which transacts itself in that upper sphere, he leaves us entirely in the dark regarding what concerns us more, appertaining as it does to the interests of the nether world. We should have liked to know, for instance, what became of the Virgin Mary, who at the cross, it will be remembered, was consigned to his protection. It would have been much more interesting if he had deigned to inform the world of the last days of the mother of God on earth, rather than have given such a sad picture of the affairs of heaven, his information in regard to which exceeds that conceded by Jesus himself, who is alleged to have resided there from all eternity ; and indeed it is marvellous that the Alpha and Omega did not inform the world on this point. It could not have been a forbidden subject, else John would not have been permitted to publish his Revelation, although he really seems better informed about what was going on in heaven than about what transpired on earth, as will be admitted when we remind our readers that he did not know that Simon Peter and his brother Andrew were his brother Apostles, brother witnesses of the word, and brothers in distress for the New Testament, who were incarcerated for preaching in the Temple together, and that he tells the believing world that these two brothers were the disciples of John the Baptist, the cousin of Jesus, who informed them that he was the Messiah. Indeed, all this is conclusive proof that this pretender John was not, as he boasts, an eye-witness of what he records and not a companion of these two Apostles, who were the disciples of John the Baptist. Surely an eye-witness and the constant companion of Jesus, nay, his bosom friend, could not possibly commit a mistake of this kind in respect to Peter; that Simon Peter to whom, as chief, Jesus had given the keys of both earth and heaven. If John has made a mistake in respect to heavenly affairs, there may be some excuse, and he has the advantage of being in a position to challenge any one to contradict him; but it was inexcusable for him to commit such a glaring blunder in earthly matters, that even we, here and now, can take demonstrable exception to his statements.

We cannot, however, accept without some criticism the information which John has given of heaven, and we will throw ourselves on the candour of our readers in asking them to endorse the justice and truth of our remarks. In the first place, we would call attention to the solemn obligation he lays upon his readers to believe his statements (Rev. i. 1) :—

"The revelation of Jesus Christ, which God gave unto him to show unto His servants things which must shortly come to pass; and He sent and signified it by His angel unto His servant John; who bare record of the word of God, and of the testimony of Jesus Christ, and of all things that he saw. Blessed is he that readeth, and they that hear the words of this prophecy and keep those things which are written therein; for the time is at hand."

This is a most solemn and impressive appeal to all mankind to accept with most absolute faith asseverations which disclose what will "shortly come to pass" as a "revelation of Jesus Christ, which God gave unto him." And yet we know, notwithstanding the appalling contrary faith of the Christian world, that the record here given is *not* true, but incarnate falsehood. And who can take exception to this conclusion when he compares the high pledge here given with the deceptive fulfilment? And yet, in chapter xxii. 19, St. John concludes with these peremptory words, "For I testify unto every man that heareth the words of the prophecy of this book, If any man shall add unto these things, God shall add unto him the plagues that are written in this book." Verily no condemnatory judgment that can be penned is more injurious to the Christian philosophy than are the productions of the four Greek writers who first introduced it to the world. Their records, solemnly written as they are, prove to be an incredible jumble of sense and nonsense, fact and fiction, and the result of critical inquiry into their worth leaves behind it an impression of amazement that writings such as these should have imposed so long on an intelligent world. Of this jumble St. John supplies a further instance in what he teaches respecting the occupation of the spirits of the just; for whereas Christianity elsewhere teaches that they are holily occupied, this is what he says he sees in heaven (chap. vi. 9–11) :—

"And when he had opened the fifth seal, I saw under the altar the souls of them that were slain for the word of God, and for the testimony which they held. And they cried with a loud voice, saying, How long, O Lord, holy and true, dost thou not judge and avenge our blood on them that dwell on the earth? And white robes were given unto every one of them, and it was said unto them, that they should rest yet for a little season, until their fellow-servants also and their brethren, that should be killed as they were, should be fulfilled."

On reading this, one is tempted to exclaim, "Verily, the best of saints make the worst of angels." Surely the spirits of the just are not worse in their disembodied than in their embodied state, and something else is to be expected than that on their translation they should of a sudden put off meekness and put on vengeance, and say, "How long, O Lord?" And yet this is the teaching of the so-called bosom friend of the Almighty, whom the credulous Christian world worshipfully designates St. John the Divine, and holds up as a paragon of human tenderness and a model

Christian disciple and father, for the admiration and veneration of all mankind.

Those who have read the preceding chapters will have in recollection the denunciation of the meek historical Jesus; we need not, therefore, repeat his utterances, but it is necessary that we should recall the attention of the reader to his principal one, in order to identify the reference made to it by John. The words of the historical Jesus are narrated by Josephus ("Book of the Wars," book vi.) : "A voice from the east, a voice from the west, a voice from the four winds, a voice against Jerusalem and the holy house, a voice against the bridegrooms and the brides, and a voice against this whole people." John had obviously before his mind this cry when he wrote Rev. vii. 1–3, "And after these things I saw four angels standing on the four corners of the earth, holding the four winds of the earth, that the wind should not blow on the earth, nor on the sea, nor on any tree. And I saw another angel ascending from the east, having the seal of the living God, and he cried with a loud voice to the four angels, to whom it was given to hurt the earth and the sea, saying, Hurt not the earth, neither the sea, nor the trees, till we have sealed the servants of our God in their foreheads."

These revelations of St. John illustrate the predictions of the historical Jesus in a manner to confirm the conclusion we have already arrived at. In the identification of him with the traditional Christ, it should not be forgotten that the age which accuses the former age of Pontius Pilate of putting in practice the *suppressio veri* is the age found guilty of the greater crime of the *suggestio falsi*. In order to prove the one it became necessary to commit the other; but in this charge we do not include the writers of the four Gospels themselves. They evidently desired to hand down truths agreeably to a particular system. If they write of the would-be prophet who was killed by Pontius Pilate, they at least refer to an actual historical character, some of whose peculiarities have not unlikely found embodiment in the character they give of the traditional Jesus; but there can be little doubt the particulars they aspire to give respect the historical Jesus of the period of the signs and wonders, the period when the Messiah was expected to appear. The history of this meek Jesus combined with that of his contemporary the Galilean supplies the main features of the subsequent narrative of the four Greek writers. Be it remembered further that our historical Jesus is represented as having the gift of prophecy. He it was, and no other known to history, who prophesied the destruction of Jerusalem. He it was who prophesied the destruction of the Temple. He it was who, in connection with these events, prophesied his own death. He it was who was arraigned before the Sanhedrim, and who suffered mockery and excoriation. He it was who was brought before the procurator, and whose bones were laid bare, as a punishment for prophesying the destruction of the Temple. He it was who was asked by the procurator who he was, and whence he came, and why he uttered such words, and who made no manner of reply to what he said.

Let those who imagine we are referring to the traditional Jesus as described by the four Greek writers know that they are mistaken, for we are speaking of the historical Jesus, the account of whom first became known to the world in the Greek of Josephus. Shortly after the completion of Josephus in Greek the Greek writings were composed, and Josephus is the only historical authority for what they say, from whose works, therefore, it is presumed the groundwork of the tradition was derived; and this discovery would have been made earlier but for the fact that the Greek writers blended two characters into one, and referred these to the prophet of the period of Pontius Pilate, with this result, that they have not produced either a perfect man or a perfect God. History is opposed to such a belief; theology is opposed to such a belief; metaphysics is opposed to such a belief; philosophy is opposed to such a belief; reason and common sense when combined, without other influences, condemn the unholy alliance as the imperfect act of man; and we pray God that it may be the last attempt to deify a brother, and set him up as a *false claimant for the throne of God.* The very idea of perfection is in this case opposed not only to the facts of history, the speculations of philosophy, and the dogmas of theology, but to all common sense and experience of the world. But this is what is to be looked for when man attempts to deify humanity and humanise divinity.

Thus have I, with such means as lay to hand, and in circumstances far from prosperous, completed, as I could, the task I had undertaken; and I now leave my statement, such as it is, in the hands of the public, not without confidence that I may gain the ear of here and there an approving critic, and in the hope that others more competent and better equipped may be induced to take up the view I have argued for, and vindicate the truth of it by an ampler and more satisfying array of proof. I have, as already hinted, only broken ground upon the subject, and done little more than indicate the lines along which, as I think, respect for history requires, criticism should in this matter proceed. Enough, I am persuaded, has been said by me to demonstrate the truth of the main features of my theory, which is all I have aimed at; and I hope I may look to others to apply to the proof of it greater range of inquiry, keenness and depth of insight, clearness of method, and comprehensiveness of grasp, and so impart to the argument greater fulness and weight. I think I have shown that the only authentic history of the period in question is that accorded by Josephus, and that the study of his pages fully warrants the conclusion that for the historical prototype, or rather prototypes, of the traditional Jesus we must look to a date later than that given in the Evangelical accounts. From this, as well as internal evidence, I have felt entitled to argue that these accounts savour largely of fiction, and that they cannot be trusted when they claim for that fiction the prerogative of God's fact. It is exactly this claim which gives to the question all its interest; and it is because, if we acknowledge that, we must forego reason, I have felt compelled to expose the untrustworthiness of the said accounts. The truth of the doctrine taught depends, as is alleged, upon the truth of the facts recorded, but as the facts are false, so therefore is the philosophy. Of this, which I and many others distrust, I find as little trace in the records of history, as in the accredited oracles of God and the postulates and corollaries of reason. The peculiar dogmatic of the Christian creed has thus not a leg to stand upon.

In calling upon the Christian world to accept the gage I throw down, I may be allowed to protest that I am not actuated by any sectarian zeal, but by a single desire to plead the claims of truth and promote the aims of charity. It is the interest of all that the grounds of the Christian dogmatic should be fairly tested, and that its truth should be sharply challenged, if its facts are false. Than this dogmatic nothing can be more alien to the Jewish faith, of which it professes to be the development. For that faith is expressly grounded on the total abnegation of all philosophy, in simple submission to the revealed will of God. Before the idea of God and the providence of God Judaism bows the head, as in the presence of an inscrutable mystery; and it cannot endure, but must by all means protest against, the stupendous assumption of Christianity, that the Absolute has sundered itself from itself and incorporated itself in meagre flesh and blood. So far from professing to know Him, it expressly declares, " His ways are in the deep, His path in the great waters, and His footsteps are not known." Nor is the Christian dogmatic alien merely to the faith of the people among whom it originated; it is equally opposed to the spirit of other religions among intelligent races, and the wisdom of the wise of all lands. " We are," says one of these last, who is not of Jewish blood, yet whose wisdom is all instinct with the spirit of Hebrew piety,—" We are as soldiers fighting in a foreign land, who understand not the plan of the campaign, and have no need to understand it; intent to know wisely and do valiantly what lies to our hand to be done." * So far as Christianity insists on this last obligation, let her voice be respected; and let all war with her pretensions cease whenever she condescends to resolve her claims to Divinity into a simple assertion of the absolute authority of reason and conscience in the life of man. Then will the point at issue between Jew and Gentile narrow itself to this :—

* Thomas Carlyle.

Which is ultimate and sovereign, the law of the letter written by the finger of God on tablets of stone given to Moses, or the law of the spirit insculpt on the thoughts and hearts of all childlike men? And this surely is an issue in regard to which reasonable people will not long contend.

THE END.

www.ingramcontent.com/pod-product-compliance
Lightning Source LLC
Chambersburg PA
CBHW031327230426
43670CB00006B/267